Guide and Reference to the Turtles and Lizards
of Western North America (North of Mexico) and Hawaii

UNIVERSITY PRESS OF FLORIDA

Florida A&M University, Tallahassee
Florida Atlantic University, Boca Raton
Florida Gulf Coast University, Ft. Myers
Florida International University, Miami
Florida State University, Tallahassee
New College of Florida, Sarasota
University of Central Florida, Orlando
University of Florida, Gainesville
University of North Florida, Jacksonville
University of South Florida, Tampa
University of West Florida, Pensacola

University Press of Florida

Gainesville · Tallahassee · Tampa · Boca Raton

Pensacola · Orlando · Miami · Jacksonville · Ft. Myers · Sarasota

Guide and Reference to the

TURTLES AND LIZARDS

of Western North America (North of Mexico) and Hawaii

R. D. BARTLETT AND PATRICIA P. BARTLETT

14 13 12 11 10 09   6 5 4 3 2 1

Library of Congress Cataloging-in-Publication Data
Bartlett, Richard D., 1938–
Guide and reference to the turtles and lizards of western North America
(north of Mexico) and Hawaii / R. D. Bartlett and Patricia P. Bartlett.
p. cm.
Includes bibliographical references and index.
ISBN 978-0-8130-3312-9 (alk. paper)
1. Turtles—Hawaii—Identification. 2. Turtles—Alaska—Identification.
3. Turtles—Canada, Western—Identification. 4. Lizards—Hawaii—
Identification. 5. Lizards—Alaska—Identification. 6. Lizards—Canada,
Western—Identification. I. Bartlett, Patricia Pope, 1949– II. Title.
QL666.C5B18 2009
597.920978—dc22   2008040284

The University Press of Florida is the scholarly publishing agency
for the State University System of Florida, comprising Florida A&M
University, Florida Atlantic University, Florida Gulf Coast University,
Florida International University, Florida State University, New College
of Florida, University of Central Florida, University of Florida, University of North Florida, University of South Florida, and University
of West Florida.

University Press of Florida
15 Northwest 15th Street
Gainesville, FL 32611-2079
http://www.upf.com

Contents

TURTLES AND TORTOISES   15

LIZARDS   67

Species

TURTLES

SNAPPING TURTLES, FAMILY CHELYDRIDAE

1. Common Snapping Turtle, *Chelydra serpentina serpentina*

MUD TURTLES, FAMILY KINOSTERNIDAE

2. Arizona Mud Turtle, *Kinosternon arizonense*
3. Yellow Mud Turtle, *Kinosternon flavescens*
4. Sonoran Mud Turtle, *Kinosternon sonoriense sonoriense*
   5. Sonoyta Mud Turtle, *Kinosternon sonoriense longifemorale*

TYPICAL SEA TURTLES, FAMILY CHELONIIDAE

6. Loggerhead Sea Turtle, *Caretta caretta*
7. Pacific Green Sea Turtle, *Chelonia mydas agassizii*
8. Pacific Hawksbill Sea Turtle, *Eretmochelys imbricata bissa*
9. Olive Ridley, *Lepidochelys olivacea*

LEATHERBACKS, FAMILY DERMOCHELYIDAE

10. Pacific Leatherback, *Dermochelys coriacea schlegelii*

BASKING TURTLES, FAMILY EMYDIDAE

11. Pacific Pond Turtle, *Actinemys marmorata*
12. Western Painted Turtle, *Chrysemys picta bellii*
13. Western River Cooter, *Pseudemys gorzugi*
14. Big Bend Slider, *Trachemys gaigeae*
15. Red-eared Slider, *Trachemys scripta elegans*
16. Ornate Box Turtle, *Terrapene ornata ornata*
    17. Desert Box Turtle, *Terrapene ornata luteola*

WHIPTAILS AND RACERUNNERS, FAMILY TEIIDAE

NIGHT LIZARDS, FAMILY XANTUSIIDAE

Quick Reference to the Turtles and Lizards of Hawaii, Alaska, and Western Canada

HAWAIIAN SPECIES

6. Loggerhead Sea Turtle, *Caretta caretta*
7. Pacific Green Sea Turtle, *Chelonia mydas agassizii*
8. Pacific Hawksbill Sea Turtle, *Eretmochelys imbricata bissa*
9. Olive Ridley, *Lepidochelys olivacea*
10. Pacific Leatherback, *Dermochelys coriacea schlegelii*
15. Red-eared Slider, *Trachemys scripta elegans*
22. Wattle-necked Soft-shelled Turtle, *Palea steindachneri*
23. Chinese Soft-shelled Turtle, *Pelodiscus sinensis*
34. Yellow-crested Jackson's Chameleon, *Chamaeleo jacksonii xantholophus*
42. Stump-toed Gecko, *Gehyra mutilata*
43. Tokay Gecko, *Gekko gecko*
44. Common House Gecko, *Hemidactylus frenatus*
45. Indo-Pacific Gecko, *Hemidactylus garnotii*
46. Mediterranean Gecko, *Hemidactylus turcicus*
47. Indonesian Tree Gecko, *Hemiphyllodactylus typus typus*
48. Mourning Gecko, *Lepidodactylus lugubris*
49. Orange-spotted Day Gecko, *Phelsuma guimbeaui guimbeaui*
50. Golddust Day Gecko, *Phelsuma laticauda laticauda*
51. Giant Day Gecko, *Phelsuma madagascariensis grandis*
65. Green Iguana, *Iguana iguana*
119. Green Anole, *Anolis carolinensis carolinensis*
120. Western Knight Anole, *Anolis equestris equestris*
121. Brown Anole, *Anolis sagrei*
123. Snake-eyed Skink, *Cryptoblepharus poecilopleurus*
124. Copper-tailed Skink, *Emoia cyanura*

125. Metallic Skink, *Lampropholis delicata*
126. Moth Skink, *Lipinia noctua noctua*

ALASKAN SPECIES

The turtles listed here are of accidental occurrence in Alaskan waters.
6. Loggerhead Sea Turtle, *Caretta caretta*
7. Pacific Green Sea Turtle, *Chelonia mydas agassizii*
9. Olive Ridley, *Lepidochelys olivacea*
10. Pacific Leatherback, *Dermochelys coriacea schlegelii*

WESTERN CANADIAN SPECIES

1. Common Snapping Turtle, *Chelydra serpentina serpentina*
6. Loggerhead Sea Turtle, *Caretta caretta*
7. Pacific Green Sea Turtle, *Chelonia mydas agassizii*
8. Pacific Hawksbill Sea Turtle, *Eretmochelys imbricata bissa*
9. Olive Ridley, *Lepidochelys olivacea*
10. Pacific Leatherback, *Dermochelys coriacea schlegelii*
11. Northern Pacific Pond Turtle, *Actinemys marmorata*
12. Western Painted Turtle, *Chrysemys picta bellii*
26. Northwestern Alligator Lizard, *Elgaria coerulea principis*
75. Pygmy Short-horned Lizard, *Phrynosoma douglasii*
76. Greater Short-horned Lizard, *Phrynosoma hernandesi*
122. Wall Lizard, *Podarcis muralis*
132. Skilton's Skink, *Plestiodon skiltonianus skiltonianus*

Preface

There is more interest today in the reptiles with which we share our world than ever before. Although the snakes are foremost in the mind of many, the lizards and the turtles are a close second. Lizards are more tolerated than snakes by herpetophobes, and the turtles are liked by almost everyone.

In addition to the professional interest of academicians and herpetologists in lizards and turtles, they become popular as pets, are the target subjects of ecotours, and are recognized as part of the world of gardeners and backyard naturalists. Herpetological clubs, reptile and amphibian expos, even herpetological seminars are held across the country and around the world. Internet chats and online pet forums are readily available to anyone with Internet access. Accurate information about the private lives of many of the more popular lizard and turtle species is now available to anyone who wishes to have it.

Herp expos vary from tiny expos, with a dozen tables and a half-dozen vendors, to the National Reptile Breeder's Convention every August in Daytona Beach, with 600+ tables of breeders/vendors.

In these pages we offer information and photos of all the lizards and turtles of the western United States and Hawaii. Introduced species are included. We hope that you'll find them all of as much interest as we do, and all worthy of further study and protection.

Keys to the Families of Turtles and Lizards

TURTLES

1a. Elongate flipperlike forelimbs 2
1b. Normal (not flipperlike) forelimbs 3
2a. Hard nonridged shell . . . **Typical Sea Turtles, Family Cheloniidae**
2b. Skin-covered carapace having longitudinal ridges . . . .
  . . . .**Leather-backed Sea Turtles, Family Dermochelyidae**
3a. Toes strongly webbed 4
3b. Toes not strongly webbed. 6b
4a. Shell hard to margins, scutes prominent 5
4b. Shell leathery, margins flexible 7
5a. Posterior marginals not strongly serrate 6
5b. Posterior marginals strongly serrate. 10
6a. Carapace high domed. 7
6b. Carapace with low, smooth dome 8
7a. Carapace high domed, feet clublike . . . .
  . . . . **Tortoises, Family Testudinidae**
7b. Carapace smooth, leathery, flexible along margin; elongate nose,
  webbed feet with 3 claws . . . .
  . . . .**Soft-shelled Turtles, Family Trionychidae**
8a. Plastron small; very long neck. . . . .
  . . . .**Snapping Turtle, Family Chelydridae**
8b. Plastron large 9
9a. No plastral hinge present . . . .
  . . . . **Basking Turtles, Family Emydidae** (in part)
9b. Plastron with one or two functional hinges. 10
10a. Plastron with one functional hinge
  . . . .**Basking (Box) Turtles, Family Emydidae** (in part)
10b. Plastron large, two functional hinges . . . .
  . . . . **Mud Turtles, Family Kinosternidae**

LIZARDS

1a. Body with lateral fold . . . . **Alligator Lizards, Family Anguidae**

1b. No lateral fold 2

2a. Limbs present. 3

2b. Limbs absent . . . . **Legless Lizard, Family Anniellidae**

3a. Functional eyelids absent. 4

3b. Functional eyelids present 5

4a. Toetips flattened and expanded. . . . .
. . . . **Typical Geckos, Family Gekkonidae**

4b. Toetips not flattened and expanded . . . .
. . . . **Night Lizards, Family Xantusiidae**

5a. Eyes lateral, protruding and turretlike, toes bundled into 2 packets
on each foot . . . . **Chameleons, Family Chamaeleonidae**

5b. Eyes and toes otherwise 6

6a. All scales shiny and in regular rows, scales not noticeably enlarged
on belly . . . . **Skinks, Family Scincidae**

6b. Scales not as above 7

7a. Dorsal and lateral scales prominent and beadlike . . . .
. . . . **Gila Monsters, Helodermatidae**

7b. Dorsal and lateral scales otherwise. 8

8a. Dorsal and lateral scales tiny and not overlapping, belly scales large
and platelike. . . . .
. . . . **Racerunners and Whiptails, Families Teiidae
and (on Vancouver Island, British Columbia only) Lacertidae**

8b. Belly scales not as above. 9

9a. Dorsal, lateral, and belly scales tiny and not overlapping . . . .
. . . . **Eyelidded Geckos, Family Eublepharidae**

9b.   Characteristics variable but not as specifically described for other
lizard families. . . . .
. . . . **Iguanas, Spiny Lizards, Horned Lizards, Earless Lizards,
and other Iguanids, Family Iguanidae**

1

Introduction

Conservationists lament development, and developers lament conservation practices. If there is a happy medium between the two, it has not yet been found.

Certainly there are now cities where wildlife once roamed, and ranches have transformed pine and oak woodlands into pastures. Favored fields and stream-drained canyons, home to many species of reptiles, fall to the ministrations of back hoes and bulldozers. And it is becoming ever-harder to find the remote outcroppings that are home to mountain kingsnakes and granite night lizards.

Though large segments may be despoiled, the western United States and western Canada remain wonderful areas. There are still areas of wilderness, montane grandeur, and remote deserts. There remain woodlands, boulder fields, scrublands, chaparral, and creosote flats. And in this region of varied topography, varied climate, varied environments, and fragmented habitats, a wonderfully varied fauna continues to exist.

Within those forests, in the deserts, and along the fog-shrouded shorelines, in the below-sea-level valleys that lie between mountains truly worthy of the term "towering," in climates that vary from uncomfortably hot along the Mexican border to close to frigid in Alaska, one can find bison, cougars, and Douglas' squirrels; condors, ravens, and lazuli buntings; polar bears and lemmings; an immense diversity of invertebrates; and the reptiles and amphibians—the "herpetofauna."

Among the reptiles are the turtles and the lizards (snakes have been addressed in volume 1 of this western series). Since the herpetofauna are ectothermic, absorbing heat from their environment, the short summers, long winters, and cold temperatures of Alaska are suitable for only a few of the most cold tolerant. But in the American west there are lizard and turtle species to fill almost every ecological niche. There are those that are secretive woodland dwellers (alligator lizards), small but very predatory desert "dragons" (the collared lizards and leopard lizards), inhabitants of montane heights (greater short-horned lizard), and a few at the opposite extreme—282 feet below sea level in the searing heat of Death Valley (zebra-tailed lizard).

And, of course, there are the sea turtles that have adapted to life in the ocean, mud turtles in seeps so small that it seems as if the turtles would have difficulty staying wet, and desert tortoises that roam the dry flats and arroyos in search of succulent vegetation to eat. You will meet all of them and more in these pages.

As might be expected, the states of New Mexico, Arizona, and California are home to most of the lizard and turtle taxa. At the opposite extreme, only a handful of species occur naturally in the northwest, Alaska, Canada, and Hawaii.

How do you go about finding lizards and turtles? The finding of many species can be defined in two words—luck and dedication!

Some species (banded geckos among them) may be rather easily found, basking on, or crossing, sun-warmed roadways, often from shortly after dusk to the wee hours of the morning. When the early morning sun begins to warm the roadway and desert you may see collared lizards or spiny lizards basking on rocks and dirt clods at road edge or on the pavement itself. Of course, if you walk rock edged desert trails you may also see collared lizards and whiptails in natural habitat. At night on rocky outcrops, with the aid of a flashlight, you may see night lizards or leaf-toed geckos. Some species are so uncommon in the United States that you may need to look often and long before actually finding them. Among these are Cope's leopard lizard, and the Baja night lizard, near the town of Jacumba, California.

Then there are, of course, two lizards that, with the desert tortoise, epitomize our southwestern deserts—the chuckwalla and the Gila monster.

The chuckwalla is a big, fat, rather slow-moving, variably colored iguanid lizard that often cannot be induced to bite, and surveys its arid-land domain from atop the loftiest of escarpments or boulders. Although the Gila monster is every bit as stocky as the "chuck," it is terrestrial—actually kind of skulking—rather than saxicolous (although it is often found in rocky desert habitats), displays a color scheme of pink and black, if molested, has an irascible disposition—and it is venomous!

DISTINGUISHING CHARACTERISTICS OF TURTLES AND LIZARDS

Let's first take a look at the turtles.

The oldest fossils of turtles appear from the Triassic Period some 248 to 206 million years ago. The creatures then appeared fully formed and identifiable as turtles; nothing is known about their actual origins.

Except for the crocodilians, the turtles (including the tortoises) are the smallest group of reptiles. Within the 13 families (give or take a couple, depending on the researcher's point of view), there are only about 75 genera and 250 species.

In the American west, western Canada, and Hawaii there are 7 families, 16 genera, and 20 species.

Of these, five species are sea turtles, one species is a land tortoise, and the rest are semiaquatic (although some are predominantly aquatic).

Turtles are unmistakable; they all have shells. The shells may vary in appearance, but they are immediately recognizable for exactly what they are—shells, formed of modified bones overlain by horny plates or by a leathery skin. The shell of an adult turtle or tortoise is more rigid than that of a hatchling.

There are the soft-edged, hard-centered shells of the various soft-shelled turtles; the streamlined, low-domed shells of the typical sea turtles; the high-domed, flat-topped shell of the desert tortoise; shells with closable plastrons (mud and box turtles); the rough-topped serrate-edged shell of the snapping turtle; and the typical shells of the rest, the basking turtles.

Turtles and tortoises are wanderers that find their food as they move about. Most species eat while under water, but the tortoises and box turtles are exceptions, feeding while out of the water.

The food items chosen by the desert tortoise are predominantly vegetable matter. Adult aquatic sliders eat submerged plants, and the oceangoing green sea turtle is particularly fond of eelgrasses. Among other things, hawksbill sea turtles eat sponges. Box turtles avidly chase down locusts and other terrestrial insects and worms. Leatherbacks seem to feed exclusively on jellyfish, and most of the other discussed species are catholic in their tastes, eating worms, crayfish, insects, fish, carrion, and plant materials. Adult snapping turtles may add frogs, smaller turtles, a duckling, or a small mammal to their menu, but they also eat a fair amount of plant material. Turtles use both visual and olfactory cues when foraging.

No matter how extensively aquatic a turtle may be, all are oviparous and all return to land to lay their eggs. A single female may deposit several clutches annually, but not all species lay every year. Hatchlings usually look at least somewhat like the adult, but are often more brightly colored.

Turtles dig nests in moist, yielding sand or dirt. The nest itself is dug with the hind feet, but some species (most notably the sea turtles) may first dig a shallow body pit with the forelimbs.

At best, construction of the nest is time consuming, but it becomes even more so if the female encounters obstructions while digging. More often than not if she encounters roots or rocks she will simply walk away from the partially dug nest to begin anew elsewhere.

Hatchlings emerge after an incubation of 55 or more days, and must then run the same gamut of predators that so often may destroy nearly an entire egg clutch. Predators include but are certainly not limited to dogs, cats, raccoons, skunks, otters, herons, gulls, snakes, other turtles, lizards, frogs, fish, crabs, and ants. Lucky indeed is the hatchling turtle that avoids all of these predators and survives to adulthood.

Interestingly, the sex of most turtles and tortoises (and some lizards, too) is determined by temperature in the nest rather than genetically. Although the precise criteria differ by species, there is a suitable ambient temperature (usually somewhere near 80–82°F) where both sexes develop, but on one side of that the clutch may develop into all males, or, on the other side, all females. Since cooler temperatures may prevail at the bottom of a nest than at the top, the turtlets at the bottom may be all one sex, those at the top all the opposite sex, and those in the center may be both sexes.

And now to the lizards.

Lizards are thought to have evolved about 315 million years ago (during the Upper Carboniferous). They have, through the ensuing eons, proven immensely successful and there are now many families, body forms, and lifestyles. Although most lizards retain legs, there are some that do not. Most have a tail that has fracture planes (breaking points) in the caudal vertebra, and the tail can be autotomized, or broken off, readily. In most cases the tail regenerates rapidly, but in some cases it does not regrow.

Reptiles may be arboreal (green iguanas and tree lizards), terrestrial (horned lizards and Gila monsters), fossorial (legless lizards and some skinks), saxicolous, that is, rock dwelling (rock lizards, some night lizards), or, in a very few cases, aquatic (marine iguanas). In fact, about the only thing lizards don't do is fly—but some (the flying dragons)—do glide. These spread patagia (gliding membranes), launch themselves from a tree trunk, and glide for long distances to another tree.

There are 16–20 families of lizards, depending on the viewpoint of the authority making the assessment. Contained within these are upward of 400 genera that comprise some 3,900 species. Of these, 14 families, 37 genera, and 110 species (all figures may vary according to the interpretations of individual researchers) occur in the American west and Hawaii.

Lizards may be herbivorous (iguanas), insectivorous (earless lizards), carnivorous (monitors), omnivorous (veiled chameleon), or vermivorous (some skinks). A few, such as the Komodo dragon, are, because of their immense size, very near the top of the food chain. Others are so small and innocuous that if they are seen at all they may be eaten by small perching birds, or even by toads and frogs.

Most lizards actively hunt their prey, depending primarily on their acute vision (racerunners and whiptails), and perhaps on their hearing or their sense of smell, to find insects and other prey.

Most lizards overcome their prey by grasping it and chewing. Even the venomous Gila monster and beaded lizard depend more on jaw strength to overcome their prey than venom. The prey is swallowed whole. Because the jaws and the body of most lizards are not capable of great distension, the preferred prey is usually small. But with that said, a few lizards have some adaptatione for eating larger prey. A lateral fold allows the body of anguid lizards to expand some, and monitors have a loose, somewhat distensible skin that also allows them to eat sizable prey items.

Unlike the snakes, comprising hundreds of dangerously venomous species, there are only two species of dangerously venomous lizards anywhere in the world: the Gila monster of southwestern United States and northwestern Mexico and the beaded lizard of Mexico and northern Central America. However, it has now been learned that, as with most of the "harmless snakes," a great many lizard species actually have certain toxic components in their saliva.

The question of whether there was really any such thing as a nonvenomous snake used to be routinely asked by the late Dr. Sherman Minton. Apparently that same question can now be echoed by current-day researchers about lizards.

The trailing by lizards of either their prey or of a reproductively active female is enabled by the tongue carrying scent particles to the Jacobson's organ in the palate. There the scents are analyzed and the trailing lizard decides what to do. Burrowing lizards may rely on vibrations and scent, more than sight, to locate prey.

Although a few snakes are capable of changing color, many lizards are, and most of those make dramatic changes; rather than camouflage, however, most of the color changes are related to stress or lack of it. Stress for lizards comes in many forms. It may be excessively cool or excessively hot temperatures, injury or fright, defense of territory from another male, or any of a number of other causes. Established male anoles, for example, may be bright green when defending their territory from an interloping male. That same male may be a warm brown when basking quietly in the morning sunlight, but quickly assume a patchy green and brown with black ear patches if it sees a snake or gets caught by a human. Male chameleons assume their most vivid colors and patterns when seeing another male, even though that second male may be 100 yards distant. Although it is the males of most lizards that assume the widest range of colors, the females of some are equally gifted.

Color change has another advantage: When emerging from a night's sleep or a winter's hibernation into the warming rays of the sun, a lizard often assumes a very dark color, the better to quickly absorb heat. As it warms, it lightens in color until, at its optimum body temperature, it is also at its most normal color.

The scales with which a lizard is covered are merely intricate folds of skin. The finished product may be smooth and shiny (like a skink), dull and bear a keel (like a spiny lizard), roughened and rasplike (like the scales of a Mauretanian wall gecko), or lengthened and platelike (like the belly scales of a whiptail). The scales may be of one or more than one color, and the interstitial skin (the skin between the scales) may be colored similarly or differently. A lizard sheds its skin at strategic times during its life. The causative agents are many and complex. Shedding is associated with growth, with the replenishment of the moisture impervious lipid barrier, and with pheromone dispersal. It may also occur at some rather well-defined times in the life of a lizard. Among these are following emergence from dormancy, prior to parturition, following an injury, or following periods of climatic change. Young, fast-growing individuals shed more frequently than old adults. For a few days prior to shedding, colors and patterns are dulled and a bluish cast may be noticeable. When the newly formed skin is suitably developed, the old epidermis is nudged free of the lips and is shed in pieces. Geckos and night lizards also shed the transparent brille (spectacle). This process is referred to as ecdysis.

Some elongate lizards, whether legless or not, may move in a sinuous, serpentine manner, pressing the outer edges of body curves against substrate irregularities. Most lizards that have legs use them in the normal manner, but if they are hurrying, they may fold the legs against their side and resort to serpentine movement.

As mentioned earlier, lizards are ectothermic. That is, their body temperature is controlled by external stimuli. To survive they must keep their body temperature between suitable temperature parameters. When their body temperature is suboptimal, lizards are affected adversely. The same holds true if they overheat. The process of controlling their body temperature is called thermoregulation. Where and when climatic conditions are so adverse that thermoregulation becomes impossible, lizards brumate (the reptilian equivalent of hibernating). This period of dormancy may last for several days, several weeks, or several months. It may be instigated by the cold, by excessive heat, or even by drought. Not all lizards have the same thermal tolerances. To successfully overwinter, a lizard must have adequate fat reserves and be well hydrated when entering brumation. While active, lizards thermoregulate by seeking shade on hot days, basking in patches of sunlight on cold days, or altering their activity periods from day to night or vice versa.

Some lizards lay eggs (oviparity); others birth live young (ovoviviparity). Not all females breed annually. Males may indulge in ritualized fights to establish breeding rights and territorial dominance. Reproductively receptive females emit pheromones that allow males to trail them, sometimes over long distances. Breeding may involve a male holding a female immobile by biting her on the nape. Prior to breeding, some stylized courtship may be indulged in. Actual breeding may occur while the male and female snakes have their tails entwined or when the tail of the male is positioned beneath or beside that of the female. If the female finds her suitor suitable, she will lift her tail and open her cloaca, allowing the intromission by one of the male's two hemipenes. Copulation may last for several minutes. To successfully breed, a lizard must have adequate fat reserves. This is especially so with females.

Most lizards lay eggs. A month or so following a successful breeding, a female of an oviparous species will lay her clutch of eggs in a protected, moisture-retaining area. Some females may produce a second clutch or even up to six clutches during the hot weather. The incubation duration for most species is between 45 and 70 days. It may take the females of live-bearing species three or four months following breeding to produce a clutch. Live-bearing species seldom multiclutch in a single season.

A NOTE ON TAXONOMY

The science of classification is called taxonomy.

As in any other discipline, there are diverging beliefs, techniques, and applications.

Because traditional systematics has "worked well" over the years, and because we feel that a field guide is not the proper forum for arguing taxonomic principles, we have continued to take a comfortable and conservative approach in these pages. Only well-accepted nomenclatural changes have been incorporated. When needed, taxonomic comments have been made in the text at the genus level of each account.

Wherever we felt it possible, both the common and scientific names used in this book are those suggested in the publication titled *Scientific and Standard English Names of Amphibians and Reptiles of North America North of Mexico, with Comments Regarding Confidence in Our Understanding*. This publication is the result of study by a panel of eminent herpetologists, chaired by Brian I. Crother.

HOW TO USE THIS BOOK

In these pages we discuss 168 species and subspecies of turtles and lizards. While many are of very dissimilar appearance, some are confusingly similar, and some are actually identical to a close relative in morphology, differing only genetically.

To add to identification problems, some of these species have two or more color phases and some (such as chameleons and anoles) may change color and pattern from one minute to the next. Because of this it can be difficult to categorize these creatures by color or pattern.

Therefore, we opted to list and discuss all in a traditional manner, divided by families, subfamilies, genera, species, and subspecies.

We further believe that a guide of this sort is not the place to attempt to justify or decry "cutting-edge" taxonomy; we have opted, for the most part, to use the tried and true, or, if new, well-accepted traditional names—both common and scientific. Future changes in both may occur.

We have fully listed and numbered all species and subspecies in a species list following the table of contents. The numbers assigned there will coincide with the numbers assigned in both text and photographs. If you know, or have a good idea what the species is you are researching, begin with the species list.

We have listed each major group, genus, species, and subspecies alphabetically by scientific name. Therefore, you may have to search some if you know only the common name of a species, including checking the index. Also, check the photo and range map provided for each species.

We have provided additional quick reference lists for Hawaiian, Canadian, and Alaskan taxa.

Scientific names are of Latin or Greek derivation. They can be binomial (two names) or trinomial (three names).

Examples of each are as follows:

• Big Bend slider, *Trachemys* (tray-chem-ees) *gaigeae* (guage-ee), a turtle species that has not subspeciated and is thus identified by only a binomial.

• Speckled earless lizard, *Holbrookia* (hole-brook-ee-ah) *maculata* (mack-you-lah-taa) *approximans* (ah-prox-ih-mans), for which the trimomial indicates subspeciation.

Let's work our way through one example:

While driving a desert road in south central Arizona, you've just encountered a small, flat lizard lying on the edge of the roadway. It's reddish tan, but the outer edges are abruptly darker than the center of its back. And it has horns on the back of its head. Well, those horns should be a dead giveaway. It's a horned lizard, but what kind of horned lizard? Turn to the species list at the front of the book and move down until you've reached horned lizards. Then turn to the section and go through it, one species account at a time. By the time you get to the account for the regal horned lizard, you will have probably begun to think the creature is not depicted, but suddenly on the page in front of you is the lizard from the roadside and the range map agrees that it is found where you saw it. Success.

While this process of elimination is certainly not scientific, it will often lead to the same conclusion that scale counts and other more formal procedures will.

ABOUT THE RANGE MAPS

When an area the size of the western United States and western Canada is reduced to a range map of some 1½ x 1½ inches in size, there is little hope for any real kind of accuracy. This is especially true when, within a region, a particular reptile may be found only in isolated patches of loose sand, along montane streams, or in other localized and specific habitats. The maps should be used only as a guide, a way to make you aware that you are somewhere close to the range of a given species or subspecies and to help you eliminate noncontending look-alikes from the list of possibilities.

TURTLES AND LIZARDS IN CAPTIVITY

Turtles and Tortoises

All of the flippered marine species and the desert tortoise are fully protected and can be maintained only with a permit.

Agencies do sometimes have desert tortoises available that they can legally offer for adoption. Check with these organizations if a tortoise happens to be *the* reptile you just can't live without.

Desert tortoises are strictly terrestrial. They are also predominantly herbivorous. To thrive they will require a large outside pen, natural sunlight, and a winter hibernaculum. Check with your adoption agency for specifics on diet and caging for tortoises.

Babies of the sliders, cooters, and other freshwater turtles of the west do very well in an aquarium with several inches of water and a brightly illuminated and warmed haul-out area. The water can be cooler than the haul-out area. In other words, like your lizards, your turtle must be able to thermoregulate. The terrarium can be as simple or as complex as you choose to make it. In the wild, babies of these turtles feed largely on insects, worms, and small gastropods. In captivity they will readily accept any good-quality prepared turtle diet as well as crickets, small worms, and other culinary delights.

Albino red-eared sliders are now being bred by hobbyists

Merely because of the large space you must provide for them, larger freshwater turtles can be difficult to keep indoors. They are more easily kept in a garden pool or similar setup. As the cooters and sliders grow, they become more herbivorous. Captive adults will do well on a diet of water plants, lettuces (no iceberg lettuce) and other greens, and a little low-fat dog chow.

Mud turtles are predominantly aquatic and do not seem to require full spectrum lighting to survive. Additionally, they are fairly small, even when adult. Adults can bite painfully, and wild ones will not hesitate to attempt to do so. Handle all carefully. Mud turtles are carnivorous throughout their lives.

Box turtles are terrestrial turtles that do best in outside garden pens, with full access to Mother Nature. Despite having a reputation for herbivory, box turtles are actually very omnivorous. They enjoy succulent worms, crickets, and carrion, as well mushrooms, berries, and some greens. Captives seem to do well on these items plus low-fat dog food with a few berries and bananas added.

Soft-shelled turtles are fully aquatic and will thrive for years in aquaria with a layer of fine sand on the bottom. It is necessary, of course, to maintain suitable water quality and to keep the substrate clean. Soft-shells readily accept live minnows (the long-term use of frozen fish seems contraindicated), worms, and some prepared foods.

It is a good idea to keep soft-shells singly. By doing so, you can more closely monitor health conditions and eliminate the possibility of them scratching one another.

Lizards

The lizards of this region run the full gamut of habitat preferences. There is much variety in habitat preference even within lizards of a given family or of closely related families. For example, while the color-changing green anole is largely arboreal, the brown anole lives low on the trunks of trees or on the ground. Some geckos live rather high on the walls of buildings or, more rarely, on the trunks of trees, but the eyelidded geckos are confirmed ground dwellers. Collared lizards prefer rocky terrain, while the leopard lizards are creatures of sparsely vegetated gravelly spaces.

To succeed in keeping your lizards, whatever the species, you will have to be aware of their habitat preferences.

Texas banded (pictured) and other banded geckos are among the most easily kept of terrestrial lizards

Provide dry quarters with climbing facilities for fence and spiny lizards, the brown anole, and skinks. The substrate can be sand, newspaper, or paper towels, or flat, dry leaves (such as those of the live oak). Skinks will prefer a few inches of dry sand or sandy loam, topped with an inch or two of dry leaves or with a flat board under which they may seclude themselves.

Provide arboreal lizards, such as the green anole, house geckos, and baby iguanas, with a vertically oriented terrarium, or at least with a spacious, tall, horizontally oriented one. Wild-caught spiny-tailed iguanas are nervous lizards that are prone to dashing into the glass of a terrarium when the cage is approached. A visual barrier such as piece of cloth or newspaper may need to be taped to the front of the cage to prevent frightening these remarkable-appearing lizards until they become used to their new restraints.

Green and spiny-tailed iguanas do well as captives, providing they are given sufficient space and a vegetable diet. Despite the fact that the iguanas of both genera eagerly eat insects and meats, there is now irrefutable evidence that diets high in animal proteins are cumulatively deleterious to their long-range health. Although a little animal protein may not hurt (especially the spiny-tails), the major portion of the diet should be vitamin-mineral–rich greens that do not contain oxalic acid (oxalic acid inhibits the metabolizing of calcium). It appears that neither green nor spiny-tailed iguanas metabolize orally given calcium well. This is especially so when they are not provided with strong, full-spectrum lighting.

Collared lizards, leopard lizards, earless lizards, zebra-tailed lizards, and fringe-toed lizards are desert speedsters that dart from rock to rock or from grass or shrub clump to the next. Their well-being depends on their ability to thermoregulate in bright, full-spectrum light. All require an illuminated hot spot in which to bask as well as a cooler area. As captives, these lizards should be provided a large horizontally oriented terrarium as well as lighting and heating that meet their requirements. Although collared and leopard lizards prey largely on other lizards when in the wild, they will adapt to a diet of insects, and, of course, insects are the natural diet of the other species mentioned.

On the subject of insects: unless the insect—whether a mealworm, cricket, locust, or roach—has been fed until almost the hour it is eaten by your lizard, your pet will be getting almost no benefit from the insect.

Gut-load your feed insects. And when feeding your lizards, provide small insects for small lizards and large insects for large ones.

Lizards and turtles can be long lived. Before taking one or more on as pets, you should consider the long-term commitment you need to make.

Turtles and Tortoises
Order Chelonia

These groups of shelled reptiles are easily recognized as turtles, but specific identification can be far more difficult.

Despite their similarities, turtles and tortoises are a diverse lot with widely varying needs and lifestyles. Contained in the 13 families, are some 75+ genera and about 250 species.

Of these, 7 families are represented by 20 species (a total of 24 subspecies) in the American west, western Canada, and Hawaii.

The terms turtle and terrapin are used differently by different folks and in different parts of the world. In the United States the term "turtle" is used for both freshwater and marine species. The terms "cooter" (of African derivation) and "slider" are also used for some of the big basking turtles in the family Emydidae. "Terrapin" is reserved by Americans for the brackish and saltwater emydines known commonly as diamondbacks (there are none of these latter in the west or Hawaii). "Tortoise" is applied to only the exclusively terrestrial species.

It is often thought that the shell makes turtles impervious to attacks and predation. Certainly the shell helps protect these creatures, but does not always succeed. Alligators routinely dine on their freshwater chelonian neighbors, and terrestrial box turtles are reportedly adversely impacted by an introduced scourge, tiny tropical fire ants. Predation by raccoons, opossums, dogs, and cats takes its toll on eggs and hatchlings. Vehicles kill many turtles as the reptiles cross highways.

Turtles colonize diverse habitats.

Sea turtles, of course, are restricted to marine environments. They are usually encountered only when females come ashore at night in the late spring, summer, and early autumn to lay their eggs. Be aware, though, that all marine turtles are classified as Endangered or Threatened, hence protected by both federal and state regulations. Their nesting activities are often monitored by watchdog groups that disallow close approach by observers.

Box turtles are open meadow, prairie, and woodland animals that may be active by day during or following showers and are especially so in the spring and early summer months. They often cross rural roadways that traverse their habitats.

Desert tortoises are creatures of the sandy ridges and swales that support the grasses and herbs on which they feed. They are active throughout much of the year.

Basking turtles are commonly seen in canals, ditches, lakes, and rivers. They are wary where persecuted for food or other reason, but are often accustomed to rather close approach in state and federal parks where they are protected.

2

Snapping Turtles

Family Chelydridae

When safely ensconced in water, these large turtles are seldom defensive and rarely aggressive. However, when they are out of the water, their attitudes can be radically different. The common snapper has a neck nearly as long as its carapace and if ashore may lunge and snap at any approaching object—your hand included. Because of the great reach and strong jaws of snappers, large individuals should be very carefully approached and handled only with the greatest of care. To move a snapper grasp it firmly by its long tail and carry it with its neck directed away from your leg (its plastron closest to your leg). The mud-brown carapace is very rough and prominently keeled.

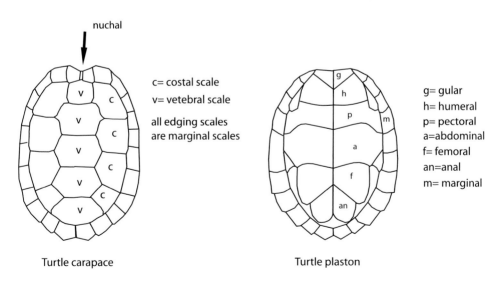

nuchal

c= costal scale
v= vetebral scale

all edging scales
are marginal scales

g= gular
h= humeral
p= pectoral
a=abdominal
f= femoral
an=anal
m= marginal

Turtle carapace   Turtle plaston

Typical turtle carapace and plastron, with scute names

The common snapper is a fecund turtle. Where soils at the nesting site are yielding, the snapping turtle often first digs a body pit to reach firmer soils and then digs the nest. More than 50 eggs can be laid. Females nest annually. Depending on nest temperature and soil conditions, hatchlings can emerge after slightly less than two months or more than four months of incubation.

Snappers, omnivorous turtles, eat all manner of smaller aquatic organisms, from insects and tadpoles to fish, carrion, and aquatic and emergent plants. They occasionally eat baby water birds and small mammals. Snapping turtles continue to be a food source for many people. They are also indiscriminately killed by fishermen who erroneously blame the beasts for depleted stocks of game fish.

Snapping Turtles: Big, and with a Bite!

Common snapping turtles, *Chelydra s. serpentina*, are too common in the eastern and central United States and in adjacent Canada to elicit much response, but that is not so in the west—at least not yet. The big, usually short-tempered aquatic turtles are native to the easternmost portions of our coverage area, but populations farther to the west are thought to be the result of introduction by humans.

At one time or another we have encountered snapping turtles throughout their eastern and central range as well as throughout their extensive Latin American range (different subspecies). But it took many trips before we met one in the American west, and it wasn't very far into the west. In fact, I encountered the 6-inch-long turtle on a canyon walk in southeastern Colorado. I had been hoping to find northern leopard frogs and barred tiger salamander larvae. The former were present, but the population was in deplorable condition. Most individuals I checked were suffering from *Aeromonas* infection and were well on their way to death. As I returned over the several miles I had walked I mulled over this sad situation. I finally reached the car and left the parking lot, again heading south into Oklahoma's panhandle. Barely a mile from the state line, in an area of pothole ponds, a small snapper was crossing the road.

Had I been back east I probably wouldn't have thought twice about the encounter, but here in the west the encounter became a noteworthy occurrence.

1. Common Snapping Turtle

Chelydra serpentina serpentina

Abundance/Range: The western extreme of this common eastern turtle's natural range is the eastern areas of Montana, Wyoming, Colorado, and New Mexico. It has been introduced to various areas further west. The snapper is now known to occur in all of the Pacific Coast states as well as Nevada and western Colorado.
Habitat: Nearly any quiet or slowly flowing and heavily vegetated body of fresh water or weakly brackish waters are acceptable homesites to this adaptable turtle.
Size: This turtle tops out at slightly more than 19 inches in carapace length, which, with tail extended and neck only partially so, adds up to a turtle with a length of well over 3 feet! The weight of an adult wild specimen can be more than 35 pounds. Captives have weighed in at more than 75 pounds. Hatchlings are a bit more than 1 inch in length.

Common snapping turtle

Identifying features: Hatchlings are rugose and chestnut to dark brown. They have a light spot on the outer edge of each marginal. Adults are somewhat smoother and olive brown to dark brown. The posterior edge of the carapace is strongly serrate. The plastron is very small and pliable. There are rounded tubercles on the head and neck. The tail is longer than the carapace, and the neck, when fully extended, is nearly as long as the carapace. The tail has a strongly serrate dorsal crest.

Adults are proportioned like the juveniles, but are less rugose.

While varying from light to dark brown in color, specimens in water high in sulphur or iron may appear whitish or rusty. If algae are growing on the carapace, the turtle can appear green.

Similar species: None in the range of this book.

ADDITIONAL SUBSPECIES

Other subspecies occur in Florida, Mexico, Central America, and northern South America.

3

Mud and Musk Turtles

Family Kinosternidae

Of the ten species of musk and mud turtles found in the United States, only three, all mud turtles, occur in the western states. These small turtles have rather highly domed, often elongate, carapaces. They are basically aquatic in habits but often occur in shallow water situations. They may wander far afield and occasionally can be encountered long distances from the nearest water source.

Mud turtles have proportionately large plastrons. The plastron has two hinges. The front lobe (consisting of the gular, humeral, and pectoral scutes) and the rear lobe (consisting of the femoral and the anal scutes) are movable.

Adult male mud turtles have a heavy, enlarged tail that is usually tipped with a curved spur.

Despite their small size, mud turtles have strong jaws and will try to bite if restrained or prodded. These turtles produce a musky exudate in glands at each side of each bridge where the skin meets the shell.

Mud turtles are not brightly colored.

They feed on aquatic insects, tadpoles, fish, worms, and carrion. They may occasionally eat some aquatic vegetation.

MUD TURTLES, GENUS *KINOSTERNON*

Adult female mud turtles lay several clutches of 1–7 eggs annually. The nesting site is usually in the soil at water's edge or in decaying aquatic vegetation. However, some nest 100 feet or farther from the water.

These turtles may be active by day, but actively forage in shallow water situations after nightfall. They may bury deeply into the mud when the water source dries, or they may search for another waterhole.

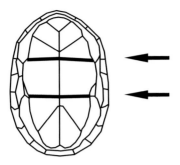

Mud turtle plastron showing hinges

Mud Turtles: Cottonwood Baskers

I had ventured southward to Quitobaquito Springs (south central Arizona) primarily to watch the pupfish. The males would be resplendent in their shimmering nuptial colors at this time of year, and that is always a big draw for me.

I parked in the lot, separated from Mexico by only a strand or two of barbed wire in need of repair.

Ahead of me, down in a little dip, was a fair-sized, cottonwood-ringed pool. A small feeder rivulet entered the pool from the east. At its widest the rivulet was all of two feet across but more often than not was only a foot or so wide. It was overhung with clumped but lush grasses for most of its way.

Zebra-tailed lizards basked on the pathway ahead of me, scuttling on hind legs into the brush when I approached too closely.

At the near end of the pool, three quarters submerged, lay a large, long-fallen cottonwood. Atop the prone trunk were two turtles. The carapace of each was dark in color—kind of an olive drab. The carapaces were high domed and elongate and seemed to be about 5 inches in length. The heads of the turtles were also dark, but there were vague light vermiculations on the cheeks. I took one more step and both turtles tumbled precipitously into the safety of the pool.

But an identification had been made. I had just met the Sonoyta mud turtle, *Kinosternon sonoriense longifemorale*, on its own turf (so to speak). The long drive to the spring had been well worthwhile.

2. Arizona Mud Turtle

Kinosternon arizonense

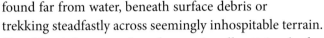

Abundance/Range: This turtle is uncommon and of limited distribution in the United States, where it occurs only in the south central Arizona counties of Cochise, Maricopa, and Pima. It is also found in Sonora, Mexico.

Habitat: This mud turtle inhabits all manner of freshwater situations. It may occasionally be found far from water, beneath surface debris or trekking steadfastly across seemingly inhospitable terrain.

Size: The Arizona mud turtle occasionally attains (or barely exceeds) 6 inches in length; 4–5 inches is the more typical length, however. Males are slightly larger than females. Hatchlings are a bit more than 1 inch long.

Identifying features: The high-domed carapace is flattened centrally. The overall carapacial color is a dark olive brown to olive tan. The marginals may be lighter in color than the rest of the carapace and often have darker smudges. Marginals number 9 and 10 (counting from the front of

Arizona mud turtle

the shell, but excluding the centermost anterior scute, the nuchal scute) are significantly higher than marginal number 8. The sutures of the first vertebral scute usually intersect the marginals at the suture of marginals 1 and 2. The head is somewhat flattened and proportionately larger in males than in females. The top of the head, neck, and limbs are usually of the same color as the carapace. The chin, cheeks, and underside of the neck and forelimbs are often yellowish or greenish. The jaws may be flecked with dark pigment. There are 2 well-developed barbels on the chin. The plastron is yellowish, olive yellow, or brownish, with each scute edged with darker pigment. This species is differentiated from the more easterly yellow mud turtle primarily by genetic data.

Similar species: The Sonoran mud turtle is of very similar appearance but has a strongly mottled head and neck. The ranges of the Arizona and the yellow mud turtle are not contiguous and do not overlap.

Comments: This turtle is often considered a subspecies of the yellow mud turtle.

ADDITIONAL SUBSPECIES

As currently recognized, none.

3. Yellow Mud Turtle

Kinosternon flavescens

Abundance/Range: This is a common turtle that occurs throughout the western two-thirds of Texas, eastern New Mexico, southeastern Arizona, and adjacent Mexico. From Texas, its range extends northward to Nebraska, and in disjunct populations, to northeastern Missouri and central Illinois.

Habitat: Like many turtles of this genus, the yellow mud turtle inhabits all manner of freshwater situations. It is often abundant in stock tanks and pothole ponds. It may occasionally be found far from water, beneath surface debris or trekking steadfastly along.

Size: Yellow mud turtles are normally 4–5 inches in length. Some may

Yellow mud turtle

attain a 6-inch length. Males are slightly larger than females. Hatchlings are about 1 inch long.

Identifying features: The high-domed carapace is flattened centrally. The overall carapacial color is olive brown to olive tan. The marginals may be lighter in color than the rest of the carapace and often bear dark smudges. Marginals 9 and 10 (counting from the front of the shell, but excluding the centermost anterior scute, the nuchal scute) are significantly higher than marginal number 8. The sutures of the first vertebral scute usually touch marginal number 2 about midway in its length. The head is somewhat flattened and proportionately larger in males than in females. The top of the head, neck, and limbs is dark. The chin, cheeks, and underside of the neck and forelimbs are yellowish. The jaws may be flecked with dark pigment. There are 2 well-developed barbels on the chin. The plastron is yellowish, olive yellow, or brownish. Each plastral scute is edged with darker pigment.

Similar species: The Sonoran mud turtle has a strongly mottled face and neck. The range of the yellow mud turtle does not overlap that of the very similar Arizona mud turtle.

Comments: The Arizona mud turtle was long considered a subspecies of the yellow mud turtle.

ADDITIONAL SUBSPECIES

As currently recognized, none.

4. Sonoran Mud Turtle

Kinosternon sonoriense sonoriense

Abundance/Range: Although still common in some parts of its rather extensive Arizona range, it is rare or extirpated from others. It now seems absent from its historic Colorado River habitats. This turtle is found from western central Arizona to southwestern New Mexico and southward into Sonora and Chihuahua, Mexico.

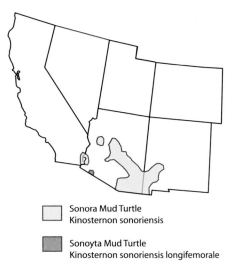

Sonora Mud Turtle
Kinosternon sonoriensis

Sonoyta Mud Turtle
Kinosternon sonoriensis longifemorale

Habitat: In the United States this turtle is associated with springs, spring runs, creeks, stock tanks, ponds, resacas, and oxbows.

Size: This large kinosternid attains an adult size of 5½ to 6½ inches. Hatchlings measure about 1¼ inch in length.

Identifying features: This turtle is seldom seen far from water, and when in the water it is often buried in mud or beneath an overhanging bank. The carapace may bear 3 keels. The carapace, head, neck, and limbs of this turtle are a warm to dark olive brown or olive gray. Carapacial scute seams may be darker. The 10th marginal is much higher than those that border it. The head, face, and neck are strongly reticulated The plastron is tan, yellow orange, or brown to tan and may bear irregular and poorly defined areas of dark pigment. The two plastral hinges are well developed. Chin barbels are prominent. Hatchlings have a rough carapace and an orange red plastron.

Similar species: Arizona and yellow mud turtles lack strong reticulations on the head and neck.

Sonoran mud turtle

ADDITIONAL SUBSPECIES

5. The Sonoyta Mud Turtle, *K. s. longifemorale*, is best identified by range. It occurs only in the Sonoyta River drainage from north of Quitobaquito Springs, Pima County, Arizona, to the vicinity of Sonoyta, Sonora, Mexico. It is differentiated from the Sonoran mud turtle by comparative measurements of the shell sutures, including a longer interfemoral seam.

Sonoyta mud turtle

4

Typical Sea Turtles

Family Cheloniidae

Four beleaguered members of this family can be found in the eastern Pacific Ocean and in the waters surrounding Hawaii. Because of more than a hundred years of exploitation, the numbers of all are reduced. Recent indications, however, indicate that the years of protection, and now the use of turtle excluders in traps and nets, are helping existing numbers to stabilize.

Several species are again breeding in increasing numbers on tropical and subtropical beaches. However, beach development continues to affect laying and hatchling behavior.

Comparatively few sea turtles nest on our Pacific Coast or on Hawaiian beaches. However, many nest in Mexico, Central America, and South America.

Females nest bi- or triennially, but in breeding years lay several clutches of 100 or more eggs at intervals through the summer. Prior to the actual nesting, a body pit is dug with the forelimbs. That done, the turtle digs the egg-chamber with her hind limbs. Incubation lasts for 2–3 months. The sex of the turtles produced in each nest is determined by the temperature within the egg chamber rather than by genetics.

Hatchlings usually leave the nest at night. They can become confused by bright lights on or behind the beach and may crawl away from, rather than to, the water.

All sea turtles have flipperlike limbs.

Two species, the loggerhead and the green turtle, are of threatened status; the hawksbill and the olive ridley are federally endangered.

Taxonomic note: There is a tendency today not to recognize any subspecies of sea turtles.

 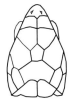 

Olive ridley   Loggerhead   Hawksbill turtle   Green turtle

Sea turtle heads showing typical scalation

Sea Turtles: Pacific Coast Rarities

Although sea turtles of both families (Cheloniidae and Dermochelyidae) are occasionally seen along the Pacific coast, none are common there. Nesting of several of the species is known to occur from central Mexico to Peru. Green turtles, hawksbill turtles, and olive ridleys may nest on some Hawaiian islands, but apparently do so very rarely. Instead they travel to, among other locations, Midway Island, French Frigate Shoals, the Leeward Islands, India, and Japan to nest. We have seen olive ridleys in rather shallow water in bays but have also seen a few far out to sea. Leatherbacks are the largest of the world's living turtles, and of the Pacific sea turtles the olive ridley is the smallest. All have flipperlike forelimbs and, except for the Pacific green sea turtle (which does haul out occasionally to bask), most do not come to shore except to breed. Because of their aquatic habits, current rarity, and protected status, it can be difficult to see marine turtles of any species. For that reason we would like to refer you to one of the nicest and most informative Web sites on Hawaiian marine turtles. Although not all species are included, there can be no doubt that the site, www.turtles.org, is a labor of love by Canadian researchers Ursula Keuper Bennett and Peter Bennett.

6. Loggerhead Turtle

Caretta caretta

Abundance/Range: Relatively common but still considered a Threatened species. This turtle may be seen anywhere along the Pacific coastline and Hawaii.

Habitat: Tropical and subtropical oceans. Strays are sometimes seen as far north as Alaska.

Size: The loggerhead may attain a carapace length of more than 3½ feet and a weight of more than 400 pounds. Hatchlings have a carapace length of 1¾ inches.

Identifying features: Following its deep brown hatchling stage, this becomes a reddish brown turtle with tan highlights. Since their color on land is often obliterated by beach sand, the true colors of this attractive turtle are the easiest to determine when the turtle is in the water. Additional clues that will help you identify this species are the following:

- five costal scutes on each side
- the first costal scute touches the nuchal scute
- usually three nonpored scutes on the bridge
- two pairs of prefrontal scales (scales between the eyelids)

Loggerhead sea turtle

Besides edible grasses (*Zostera*, etc.) loggerheads consume shellfish, crustaceans, coelenterates, fish, and myriad other marine creatures.

Similar species: No other marine turtle is a warm reddish brown. Hawksbills are darker brown or have calico carapacial scutes and only 4 costal scutes. Pacific green turtles have only a single pair of prefrontal scales and only 4 costals. Ridleys are comparatively small, olive gray or gray in color, and have 4 pored bridge scutes on each side.

ADDITIONAL SUBSPECIES

None.

7. Pacific Green Turtle

Chelonia mydas agassizii

Abundance/Range: This turtle is uncommon along the Pacific coast but common in Hawaii.

Habitat: This is an herbivorous species of open tropical and subtropical oceans. It sometimes strays far northward.

Size: This gigantic marine turtle is exceeded in maximum size only by the leatherback. Green turtles are adult at 3–4½ feet in carapace length.

Pacific green sea turtle. Photo by Ursula Keuper-Bennett and Peter Bennett

They occasionally attain a length of 5 feet and a weight of more than 500 pounds. Hatchlings are about 2 inches in length.

Identifying features: Adult Pacific green turtles have an olive brown or olive green carapace that often narrows noticeably above the hind legs. Radiating dark lines may be visible on the carapacial scutes of some of the lighter specimens. There are 4 costal scutes on each side. The first costal is *not* in contact with the nuchal scale. The venter is light. Hatchlings are dark brown to nearly black with the flippers neatly edged in white.

This species has only a single pair of prefrontal scales (the scales between the eyelids).

Similar species: All other sea turtles of this family found in Pacific or Hawaiian waters have two pairs of prefrontal scales.

Comments: In recent years green turtle populations have been plagued by rapidly developing viral fibropapillomas. It is thought that susceptibility to these viral growths may be enhanced by various pollutants to which all sea life is now subjected. A great deal of research is now directed toward this problem.

ADDITIONAL SUBSPECIES

There is an Atlantic race of this turtle.

8. Pacific Hawksbill

Eretmochelys imbricata bissa

Abundance/Range: Rarely seen on the Pacific coast, the Pacific hawksbill is more commonly encountered in Hawaiian waters.

Habitat: This is a species of the open ocean.

Size: This is a rather small sea turtle. Adults range from 28 to 32 inches long. The record size is only 36 inches. Most hawksbills weigh 100–175 pounds. Hatchlings are about 1½ inches long.

Identifying features: The carapace of the hawksbill is brown(ish), often with a prominent tortoiseshell pattern. There is a vertebral keel. The carapacial scutes are usually imbricate (overlapping). The plastron is cream to light yellow in color. Plastral keels are continuous. Young are quite similar to the adults in color but usually have a more vividly contrasting carapacial pattern. Hatchlings are very dark brown to nearly black and lack carapacial markings. This species has a narrow hawklike beak. Limbs and

Pacific hawksbill sea turtle. Photo by Ursula Keuper-Bennett and Peter Bennett

head are usually very dark, but some yellow interstitial skin may be visible between the head scales. Hawksbills feed on algae and other vegetation as well as on sponges, molluscs, crustacea, and myriad other marine creatures.

Similar species: This is the only sea turtle of the Pacific with 4 costal scutes on each side and four prefrontal scales.

Comments: The carapacial scutes of this turtle were once used extensively in the manufacture of tortoiseshell for glasses frames and other items. Fortunately plastic has replaced real tortoiseshell.

ADDITIONAL SUBSPECIES

There is an Atlantic race of this turtle.

9. Olive Ridley

Lepidochelys olivacea

Abundance/Range: This rare turtle is seen as a stray both in coastal Pacific and Hawaiian waters.

Habitat: This oceangoing turtle is more common elsewhere than in the

Olive ridley sea turtle. Photo by Sean McKeown

regions covered by this guide. It occurs in both the tropical Pacific and the tropical Atlantic.

Size: The olive ridley is a small sea turtle. It is adult at 20–25 inches. Its average weight is about 90 pounds. Hatchlings are about 1½ inches long.

Identifying features: Hatchlings are a rather uniform greenish gray with a lighter stripe on the trailing edge of each front flipper. Adults are olive green to olive yellow above and yellowish ventrally. There are usually 6 pairs of costals, 2 pairs of prefrontal scales, and either 4 (usually) or 5 (rarely) pored scutes on the bridge.

Similar species: Green turtles have only one pair of prefrontal scales. The Pacific hawksbill has 4 costals on each side. Loggerheads have only 3 scutes (nonpored) on the bridge.

ADDITIONAL SUBSPECIES

None.

5

Leatherbacks

Family Dermochelyidae

This oceangoing behemoth is the largest extant turtle. A carapace length of more than 6 feet and a weight of more than a ton have been recorded. This family has been erected solely for this divergent turtle.

Like all marine turtles, the leatherback has flipperlike limbs. Unlike other marine turtles, the leatherback has osteoderms, platelets of bone, embedded in the skin.

The leatherback is a wide-ranging turtle that is capable, because of circulatory modifications, of sustaining a warm body temperature in very cold waters. When disturbed or injured, leatherbacks have been known to attack boats. They are immensely powerful, and extreme care should be used when observing them.

This, the largest turtle in today's world, is adapted to eat jellyfish. Deaths of even large individuals have occurred after the turtles have mistaken discarded clear plastic bags for their coelenterate prey.

This immense turtle first digs a body pit with the foreflippers, then a nesting cavity with the rear flippers. They nest above the high-tide line on open beaches. Several clutches of 150+ eggs may be laid by a female during her nesting year; however, a female may nest only every two or three years. Incubation takes 2½–3½ months.

10. Pacific Leatherback

Dermochelys coriacea schlegelii

Abundance/Range: This rare and endangered turtle is occasionally seen in waters along the Pacific Coast but is more commonly seen in Hawaiian waters.

Habitat: This is a pelagic marine species about which very little is known.

Pacific leatherback. Photo by Karl Heinz Switak

Size: Most specimens seen are in the 3½–5 foot carapace range; however, the species is known to reach 6 feet 2¼ inches. Hatchlings are about 2¾ inches in carapace length.

Identifying features: The carapace and skin are slate blue to black. Adults have no plates on the carapace. There are scattered white, yellowish, or pinkish markings. There are seven pronounced longitudinal keels on the carapace. The plastron is lighter than the carapace in color. Males have variably concave plastrons. Adult females tend to have pinkish markings on the top of the head. These may or may not be present on males. The front flippers are proportionately immense. The forelimbs of the Pacific race are proportionately shorter than those of the Atlantic race. Hatchlings, which are shaped much like a keeled torpedo (the immense foreflippers being the "stabilizers"), have a ground color quite like the adults but have numerous small (often white) scales (which are later shed), white keels, and white coloration outlining both front and rear flippers.

Voice: When disturbed or injured, leatherbacks are capable of emitting sounds that are reminiscent of a human belch.

Similar species: None.

ADDITIONAL SUBSPECIES

There is an Atlantic race that is of very similar appearance.

6

Basking Turtles

Family Emydidae

The basking turtles are represented in the American west and in Hawaii by six species and total of eight subspecies. With the exception of the two subspecies of terrestrial box turtles, all others in these regions are primarily aquatic.

Most of the basking turtles in the west occur along the edges of this vast territory; the interior deserts are largely turtle free.

Rather than being genetically determined, the sex of many turtle species is determined by incubation temperature. Females are produced at higher incubation temperatures, males at lower ones. Thus, poorly positioned nests may produce turtlets of all one sex.

In many cases the colors and patterns on the upper shell (the carapace) will help in the identification of a turtle. These colors and the pattern may be dull and almost indiscernible when a turtle is dry, but more apparent when the turtle is wet. The colors and patterns are almost invariably more distinct on young turtles than on old adults.

Emydines: The Baskers

Compared with the many species of emydine (basking) turtles found in the central and eastern states and provinces, there is a paucity of emydine species exists in the west. In fact, there are only six species (eight subspecies), and of these about half have very limited natural ranges.

J. P. Stephenson had taken Gary Nafis and me out on a garter snake photographing trip. As it turned out, we saw much more than just garter snakes. In fact, J.P. took us to areas that abounded in alligator lizards, skinks, rattlesnakes, gopher snakes, racers, sharp-tailed snakes, as well as the targeted garter snakes. All were present and some were seen in fair numbers.

It was during a search for mountain garter snakes that we came to the edge of a stream-fed pasture pond of about an acre in size. In there we found not only the desired garter snakes but several individuals of a bonus species, the Pacific pond turtle, *Actinemys marmorata*, as well.

These pond turtles were, like all other examples of the species I had encountered, very wary and almost impossible to approach closely. That really wasn't a problem, for we had seen them clearly enough to be able to count them on our trip list.

Pacific pond turtles are not brightly colored. In fact, they are anything but, being olive gray to olive brown with darker radiating lines dorsally. The plastron is yellow with dark blotches. The skin is nearly the same color as the carapace.

Because of habitat reduction and the fact that pond turtles were once collected in some numbers for the pet trade, populations of both the southern and the northern pond turtles are noticeably reduced and both are now protected.

This habitat was of interest to me, for it actually was a pond. More often than not, when I have seen this species it has been in a stream.

The generic name of *Actinemys* was only recently bestowed on this turtle. Prior to this it was grouped with spotted, wood, and bog turtles in the genus *Clemmys*. Today only the spotted turtle remains in the latter genus.

PACIFIC POND TURTLE, GENUS *ACTINEMYS*

Until very recently, this turtle was, along with three eastern species, contained in the genus *Clemmys*. However, the Pacific pond turtle was sufficiently divergent for a new genus specifically for it. Although the species was traditionally divided into two races, a northern and a southern, the characteristics used to differentiate the races were not constant. Additionally, molecular studies completed in 2005 have invalidated the subspecific designations.

This is a very aquatic turtle that prefers heavily vegetated ponds but may also be found in some creeks. It hibernates in the water.

Pond turtles are considered "cool weather" turtles. They become active very early in the year, may become largely inactive during the hottest days of summer, and are again active in the autumn.

Females produce one or two clutches of 2–12 eggs. The incubation period is 58–75 days.

This omnivorous turtle species eats aquatic vegetation as well as all manner of aquatic invertebrates, tadpoles, fish, and carrion.

Wild populations of Pacific pond turtles have declined in many parts of their range. Among other things, this may be attributed to habitat fragmentation, habitat loss, collection for various reasons, and death on the roadways. The pond turtle is now a protected species.

11. Pacific Pond Turtle

Actinemys marmorata

Abundance/Range: Although still rather common in some areas, overall the populations are diminished. This turtle ranges from southwestern British Columbia, where there is a small isolated population, southward to northern Baja California.
Habitat: The pond turtle inhabits ponds, marshes, ditches, and creeks.
Size: The pond turtle is adult at 5–7 inches in length. Occasional examples may attain a shell length of 8½ inches. Hatchlings are about an inch long.
Identifying features: The carapace is light gray, olive tan, or olive gray to nearly black in color. Lighter radiating streaks

Pacific pond turtle, adult

Pacific pond turtle, juvenile

are present in all carapacial scutes including the marginals. The head and neck are olive tan to gray with dark mottlings and streaking or, conversely, primarily dark with light markings. The plastron is yellowish but usually bears dark pigment along the scute seams and on the bridges. The limbs are dark olive with obscure darker markings. The hind feet are fully webbed. Some individuals have a pair of small wedge-shaped inguinal scutes on the posterior portion of the bridge.

Similar species: Western painted turtles are much more colorful. They are patterned with bright red markings on the submarginal scutes.

PAINTED TURTLES, COOTERS, AND SLIDERS, GENERA *CHRYSEMYS*, *PSEUDEMYS*, AND *TRACHEMYS*

These are three closely allied genera. They are small to large pond and river turtles. All are persistent baskers that slide or drop into the water at the first sign of disturbance. The females are often larger than the males. The males of some species have elongated front claws that are used during their aquatic courtship rituals.

Babies are brightly colored (usually green or olive gray with both lighter and darker carapacial markings); adults are usually less colorful. Old adult males of some species become suffused with pattern-obliterating melanin and may look virtually black or olive black. The heads and necks of most are strongly striped.

Identification of the many eastern species may be problematic, but differentiating the four types in the west should pose no problem.

A single species, the red-eared slider, has been introduced to Hawaii. In fact, because of the release of unwanted pets, the popular red-eared slider has become the most widely distributed turtle in the world. Besides the Mississippi drainage (to which it was native), it occurs virtually throughout the United States, in France, Japan, Australia, and other countries as well.

Sliders and cooters have clutches of 4–20 or more eggs. Most females lay 2–4 clutches annually. Hatchlings emerge following an incubation of 58–75 days.

Hatchlings and young specimens of these turtles are largely insectivorous, but larger specimens are primarily herbivorous.

Females may take five or more years to attain sexual maturity. Males do so in about three years.

12. Western Painted Turtle

Chrysemys picta bellii

Abundance/Range: This turtle is abundant throughout much of its extensive range. It occurs in suitable aquatic habitats from Washington state and southern Canada to New Mexico, and from southwestern Ontario to Missouri.

Habitat: The western painted turtle utilizes ponds, marshes, lakes, and slowly flowing rivers for its habitat.

Size: While specimens of 4–5 inches are commonly seen, occasional adults of this turtle attain more than 9 inches. Hatchlings are about 1 inch long.

Identifying features: This turtle has a smooth greenish carapace patterned with dark-edged lighter green lines. The marginals are nonserrate and have yellowish lines flanking a vertical red central bar. The plastron is yellow to red with an extensive dark plastral figure. The head, neck, and limbs are dark. Yellow lines pattern the head. These lines shade to red on the neck. Limb markings may be yellow or reddish. Both sexes are colored similarly. Hatchlings usually have a bright red plastral ground color.

Similar species: Red-eared sliders have the namesake red ear stripe. Western river cooters have serrate posterior marginals. Pacific pond turtles lack red markings.

Western painted turtle

13. Western River Cooter (Rio Grande River Cooter)

Pseudemys gorzugi

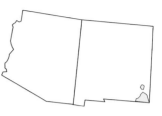

Abundance/Range: This beautifully colored turtle is common in suitable stretches of the Rio Grande and Pecos River drainages. The two populations are separated by 100 or more miles. The range of this turtle extends southward into adjacent Mexico and northward along the Pecos into southwestern New Mexico.

Habitat: The western river cooter is restricted in range to the permanent, nonpolluted stretches of the two watercourses in which it occurs. It is also found in some of the permament lakes and ponds associated with those river systems.

Size: This heavy-shelled turtle is adult at 7–9 inches in length. It occasionally attains a length of 10 inches. Females average about an inch longer than the males. Hatchlings measure about 1½ inches in carapace length.

Identifying features: Hatchlings have a green carapace busily patterned with dark blotches. The plastron is yellow with an extensive, dark, seam-

Western river cooter

following figure. The green head and legs are brightly marked with yellow.

Adults are duller but retain an intricate carapacial pattern. The carapace has a ground color of medium olive to olive brown and a pattern of curved yellow(ish) and dark olive lines surrounding yellow-centered black blotches. The rear margin of the carapace is strongly serrate. The second costal is patterned with, among other markings, a rearward directed C. Submarginal markings are in the form of ocelli. Aged specimens become suffused with pattern-obscuring melanin. The plastron is yellow(ish), and the dark juvenile pattern fades with age. Head, neck, and limbs are dark green. The head and neck have numerous, thin, bright yellow stripes and a wide oval to elongate postorbital blotch on each side. The limbs and tail are lined with yellow and/or orange (or rose). The upper jaw is smooth, bearing neither a central notch nor flanking cusps. Males have long foreclaws.

Similar species: Both the western painted turtle and the red-eared slider have smooth posterior marginals. Both the red-eared slider and the Big Bend slider have one or two red blotches behind the eyes.

14. Big Bend Slider

Trachemys gaigeae

Abundance/Range: This, the "red-eared slider" of the western Rio Grande, may be seen sunning in numbers on hot spring and summer mornings. It is found from the Big Bend region of Texas northward to central New Mexico. Hybridization with the red-eared slider may be occurring in some areas.
Habitat: The Big Bend slider requires areas of permanent water. It may be seen in the Rio Grande and in associated pools, ponds, impoundments, and cattle tanks along the river. This turtle may wander from pool to pool as the river depth lessens during periods of drought and pools dry. It may be seen sunning on banks as well as on projecting rocks, snags, and plant mats. This (and other bask-

Big Bend slider, adult

Big Bend slider, hatchling

ing turtles) may also thermoregulate by merely floating on the surface of the water.

Size: The Big Bend slider is adult at from 4½–8 inches carapace length. Adult males are usually somewhat smaller than the females. Hatchlings are about 1⅛ inches long.

Identifying features: Hatchlings of the Big Bend slider have carapaces of olive gray patterned with numerous curved lines. Two red spots, a small postocular and larger temporal spot, usually oval or rounded, are present on each side of the head. The olive green head, neck, and limbs are vividly striped with yellow. The plastron has a large, dark, central figure that follows nearly the entire midline and has outward extending arms along the scute seams.

Colors and pattern dull with age. An age-related suffusion of melanin may render some old males devoid of pattern and nearly a uniform dark olive to olive black in color.

Males of this species do not develop elongated front claws.

Similar species: Throughout most of their range, red-eared sliders have only a single, broad, elongate red ear stripe. In south Texas, where the ear stripe is quite apt to be broken into a small postorbital and a larger temporal marking, the red-eared slider has plastral ocelli (rather than the large central figure) and vertical bars (rather than curved lines) on the carapacial scutes.

Comments: The Big Bend slider was long confused with the red-eared slider, and was initially thought to be a subspecies of the latter. Most researchers now consider the Big Bend slider a full species.

The courtship sequence of the Big Bend slider differs markedly from that of the superficially similar red-eared slider. Lacking the elongated foreclaws with which the male red-ear vibrates and strokes the face of the female, the male Big Bend slider merely chases the female through the water nipping at her shell, tail, and hind legs. Breeding occurs when the female becomes quiescent.

15. Red-eared Slider

Trachemys scripta elegans

Abundance/Range: This common pond slider is now found throughout most of the United States. In the west it is found in eastern New Mexico, southern Arizona, in several places in southwestern California, near Seattle, Washington, and at other western locations. It has long been established on Oahu, Hawaii.

Habitat: The red-eared slider is common to abundant in the heavily vegetated ponds, lakes, canals, ditches, oxbows, and other such bodies of water throughout its range.

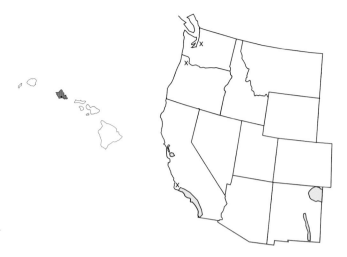

Size: Typically these pretty turtles attain an adult length of 5–8 inches. Some exceed 10 inches. Adult males are usually somewhat smaller than the females. Hatchlings are about 1⅛ inches in shell length.

Identifying features: Hatchlings of the red-eared slider have carapaces of green patterned with numerous narrow lighter and darker lines. A vertical yellow bar is present in each costal scute and on at least some of the marginals. The submarginal and plastral scutes are patterned with irregular

Red-eared slider

dark ocelli. The rear marginals are weakly serrate. The face and limbs are green with numerous yellow stripes. The very broad red temporal stripe (often broken into two spots in extreme south Texas), from which this turtle takes its name, is usually prominently evident.

Colors and pattern dull with age. Males are often duller than females of a similar age. Old males can be entirely devoid of pattern and nearly a uniform dark olive to olive black in color.

Sexually mature males have elongate front claws.

Similar species: The Big Bend slider has 2 red spots on each side of its face but has curved light markings rather than vertical bars in each costal and marginal scute. Additionally, the plastron of the Big Bend slider bears a large dark figure rather than ocelli.

Comments: For seven (or more) decades, the red-eared slider has dominated the pet trade in baby turtles. It is the little "green" or "painted" turtle that was once seen in the pet departments of nearly every five-and-dime and pet shop in the United States. Federal health regulations have now curtailed its availability somewhat, but it is still readily available commercially to those who want it. We urge, should you decide to have any turtle as a pet, that you realize this can be a lifelong commitment (your life as well as that of the turtle) and that you never turn it loose. Find it another home if necessary, but don't release it into the wild.

BOX TURTLES, GENUS *TERRAPENE*

These are terrestrial turtles with high-domed carapaces. They may occasionally enter puddles or cattle tanks to drink. It seems, however, as if at least some of the box turtle's moisture requirements are metabolized from the food eaten. Although this turtle may opportunistically eat fruit and some vegetation, it strongly prefers insects to plant matter. The desert box turtle is most active during and following rains. Over much of its range, this turtle hibernates from late October to March. Mating occurs primarily in the spring, shortly following the turtles emergence from hibernation, but may also occur in the summer and autumn of the year. Egg-laying occurs in the spring and summer months and well-nourished females may lay a second clutch. From 1 to 6 (occasionally to 8) eggs are laid at each nesting. Depending on temperature and ground moisture levels, incubation can take from 52 to more than 120 days. Immature specimens are only rarely found.

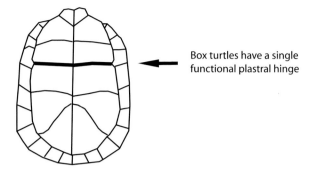

Box turtles have a single functional plastral hinge

Box turtle plastron showing hinge

16. Ornate Box Turtle

Terrapene ornata ornata

Abundance/Range: This is still a common box turtle throughout most of its range. It is most active on warm, rainy mornings, but will emerge from hiding during or following any drought-breaking storm. Within the range of this guide, the ornate box turtle may be found only in the easternmost regions of New Mexico, Colorado, and Wyoming. From these states it ranges eastward to Indiana and Louisiana.

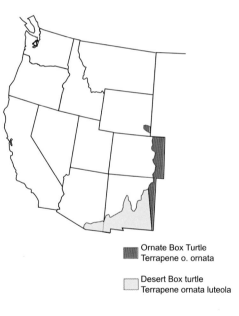

■ Ornate Box Turtle
Terrapene o. ornata

□ Desert Box turtle
Terrapene ornata luteola

Habitat: The ornate box turtle is associated with semiarid and arid grasslands and open scrub areas. It burrows into the earth, often against the trunk of a shrub, to partake of shade and to slow moisture loss. During the hottest weather, these turtles typically forage early in the day and at dusk.

Size: Adult ornate box turtles measure between 4 and 5 inches in carapace length. An occasional example may attain 5½ inches. Hatchlings are about 1¼ inches long.

Ornate box turtle

Identifying features: The adult ornate box turtle has a deep brown to olive black or black carapace with 5–9 yellowish radiating lines on the second costal. The other costal scutes are also prominently patterned with radiating lines. This race is invariably well patterned and the pattern does not fade with age. The carapace is highly domed but flattened centrally. The top of the head and the cheeks may be quite dark. The neck is usually lighter. The cheeks and neck are patterned with lighter markings. The mandibles and chin are yellowish. Orange scales are usually present on the limbs. Males often have red eyes; those of the females are yellowish. The plastron is usually dark with many light lines. The plastral hinge is well developed. Adult males have a plastral concavity on the rear lobe. The tiny tail may be yellow dorsally. Adult males have the innermost toe on each hind foot thickened and affixed at an angle to the other claws.

Hatchlings have a dark ground color with rather bright yellow spots on the carapacial scutes and a yellow vertebral stripe.

Similar species: The desert box turtle (next account) is paler and has a busier pattern. Mud turtles have 2 plastral hinges.

ADDITIONAL SUBSPECIES

17. The adult Desert Box Turtle, *Terrapene ornata luteola*, has an olive brown, olive tan, or yellowish carapace with many lighter radiating markings on each costal scute, for example, 10–16 on the second costal. The light markings may become obscure with advancing age. The top of the head may be quite dark, but the cheeks and neck are usually lighter and have tan to yellowish markings. The mandibles and chin are light, and yellowish scales are usually present on the limbs. Males often have red eyes; those of the females are yellowish. The plastron reverses the carapacial scheme, being predominantly light with many dark lines. Hatchlings of the desert box turtle bear yellow spots (and no stripes) on their tan to brown carapace and have a relatively low dome and an undeveloped plastral hinge.

The desert box turtle is found from western Texas to southeastern Arizona. It is also found in northern Mexico.

Desert box turtle

7

Tortoises

Family Testudinidae

Although this is a fairly large family, only three species—one each in the southeast, the south central, and the southwest—are found in the United States. These three, plus a single northern Mexican species, make up the genus *Gopherus*.

All are now depleted in numbers and are protected throughout their ranges.

DESERT TORTOISE, GENUS *GOPHERUS*

Tortoises have flattened forefeet with which they make burrows or sleeping depressions. The hind feet are stubby and elephantlike. The carapace is high domed and often strongly sculptured with growth annuli in each scute. A gular extension—an anterior projection used to batter and overturn rivals in territorial disputes—is present and well developed on the desert tortoise.

The desert tortoise may dig a long burrow in which it spends inclement weather, but also utilizes shallow sleeping pallets against the trunk of a shrub or other desert plant.

This species is terrestrial and is predominantly a vegetarian.

As the temperatures change seasonally, so, too, do the activity patterns of these tortoises. They are active even at midday when temperatures are moderate, but are usually active only in the cooler morning or afternoon hours during periods of excessive heat. They may hibernate, or become periodically dormant, during the worst of the winter cold.

Tortoises are slow to reproduce and have high hatchling mortality. Males are very territorial, and during the breeding season lengthy skirmishes may occur. Combat between males can last for nearly a half an hour and may result in the weaker (or unluckier) male being overturned. If this happens in an open area on a sunny day, it may result in the death of the overturned tortoise before it can right itself. June, July, August, and September are the principal months for nesting. Breeding male tortoises produce a clucking sound. Up to 14 eggs may be laid by female desert tortoises in their prime. Two or three nestings in a season have been documented. Incubation takes between 3 and 4 months.

These tortoises are colonial. All have a home territory and either a sleeping pallet or a burrow that may measure from only a foot in length to more than 30 feet, to which they regularly return.

Numerous other reptile and amphibian species use desert tortoise burrows for refugia. Longevity of these tortoises is known to be more than half a century.

An upper respiratory ailment of unknown origin, but seemingly readily spread, is now afflicting many wild desert tortoises.

Tortoises: A Desert Landlubber

Although they are now so reduced in numbers that they are protected throughout their range, it is still very possible to see a desert tortoise, *Gopherus agassizii*, in the field.

With both Randy Babb and Kenny Wray I have happened across these big dwellers of the southwestern aridlands in southeastern California and southern Arizona. In most cases they were plodding methodically across the desert, stopping here and there for a bite of succulent—or not so succulent—vegetation, but were in other places either hunkered tightly in against the base of a desert shrub or sitting quietly at or near the mouth of their burrow.

There are times when these tortoises wander some distance from their pallets or dens. Not only have we seen them grazing on grasses and succulents along the edges of busy roadways, but one evening, as Patti and I stood marveling at the grandeur of the desert landscape surrounding us on Ajo Mountain in Organ Pipe National Monument (including a fat tarantula), a large desert tortoise trudged into view. It had come from out of the dense scrub on one side of the roadway and quietly munched its way, pausing every few paces to take another bite

continued

of vegetation, across the road, until it disappeared into the scrub on the distant side.

No rush, no fuss, no hesitation; the tortoise was simply making the most of its slow but apparently deliberate wandering. Although I didn't follow it to find out, I've often wondered whether it was headed back to its home pallet for the night or merely still foraging.

18. Desert Tortoise

Gopherus agassizii

Abundance/Range: The desert tortoise ranges from southern Nevada and immediately adjacent southwestern Utah to southeastern California, western Arizona, and then southward to northern Sinaloa, Mexico. Within its range it is now of spotty distribution.

Habitat: Look for this desert denizen in sandy open scrub habitats, in cholla-sagebrush associations, near springs, in riparian habitats, near stock tanks, and on creosote-dominated flats. It may be found in rock regions, or in desert habitats with compacted sand banks into which it can burrow. This species occurs at elevations up to 5,200 feet.

Size: This tortoise has a high-domed, but flat-topped carapace. While it is normally 10–13 inches in length, occasional examples may attain a shell length of 16 inches. The hatchlings average about 1⅝ inches in carapace length.

Identifying features: Adult desert tortoises are an unrelieved brown, grayish brown, horn, or almost black. Hatchlings have a light-colored head and limbs, and their dark carapacial scutes have peach or yellowish colored centers. Prominent growth annuli are usually present, but the carapace may be worn smooth on old specimens. The plastron is usually somewhat lighter than the carapace in color. The gular projection is long

Desert tortoise

and especially well developed on adult males. The head is rounded and the neck is fairly short.

Similar species: None in our region.

Comments: Habitat degradation and other pressures have impacted the populations of this tortoise. The communicable respiratory ailment mentioned earlier is present in many tortoise colonies. This apparently can be spread by humans handling tortoises, and perhaps by animals moving between colonies. The desert tortoise is now protected throughout its range, but adoption programs for injured or captive-produced desert tortoises are in place.

ADDITIONAL SUBSPECIES

None.

8

Soft-shelled Turtles

Family Trionychidae

Two species of soft-shelled turtles, the smooth and the spiny, are represented in the American west, and two additional species, the wattle-necked and the Chinese, occur in Hawaii.

Soft-shelled turtles are almost fully aquatic. They are powerful and agile swimmers that have fully webbed feet. Besides normal pulmonary respiration, oxygen-carbon dioxide exchange occurs through the skin and mucous membranes, allowing these turtles to remain submerged for extended periods. Following hatching and prior to dispersal, hatchlings may be found in the shallow waters at the edge of sandbars. Soft-shells are adept at burying themselves in the sand in water shallow enough to allow the snout and eyes to break the surface when the turtle's long neck is extended.

These turtles are predominantly carnivorous, eating all manner of invertebrates as well as fish, amphibians, and carrion. Some vegetation may be eaten.

Soft-shells often bask while sitting in sun-warmed, shallow water, or by floating at the surface of deeper water. Soft-shells may also haul out on snags and smooth banks to bask.

Collectively, soft-shells have a long neck, a Pinocchio nose, strong jaws, and sharp claws. Large specimens must be handled carefully. With advancing age, females of most species assume a carapacial color and pattern different from that of young females and the males. The females of most species are also considerably larger than males.

Sex determination seems to be genetically, rather than temperature, determined.

Riverine soft-shells often nest on exposed sandbars. Water is almost always visible from the nesting site. Pond-dwelling forms nest on exposed banks. Nests may contain 6–40 or more eggs but a clutch is usually between 8 and 20 eggs. Following an incubation period of somewhat more than two months, the hatchlings emerge. A female lays several clutches a summer.

Soft-shells have a rounded or oval carapace (when viewed from above) that is covered with a thick, leathery skin rather than keratinized scutes. Although the center of the shell is comparatively rigid, the edges of the carapace are flexible. There are only three claws on each of the fully webbed feet. Males have a greatly enlarged tail that extends well beyond the edge of the carapace.

Soft-shelled Turtles: Swimming Flapjacks

Compared with the large numbers of Texas spiny soft-shelled turtles, *Apalone spinifera emoryi*, found basking along Texas' Rio Grande River on a hot summer day, the few we saw in the Imperial Valley canal seemed a minuscule number.

On the muddy banks of the Rio Grande, softies bask in ranks, sometimes one atop another. In this canal we had seen only three examples, but this was enough to enable us to list the turtle as a California resident that had been introduced at some point.

Soft-shells are the least turtle-like of North America's freshwater turtle fauna. Rather than plates, they have an undivided leathery covering

continued

over the bone and cartilage of their shell, and the shell has pliable edges. They have powerful legs with fully webbed feet that bear claws on three of the toes. The neck is long and very supple and the Pinnochio-like nose allows these aquatic turtles to breathe without ever showing their head or body contours.

Despite this flapjack-like countenance, soft-shells have very strong jaws and don't hesitate to bite when they are restrained.

Although the Texas spiny soft-shell seems to prefer rivers, it readily moves into irrigation canals and connected ponds. The turtles seek areas with a soft bottom in which they can easily bury themselves, but where the water is still shallow enough for them to breathe by the simple expedient of extending the long neck upward and allowing the tip of the snout to break the water's surface.

AMERICAN SOFT-SHELLED TURTLES, GENUS *APALONE*

These are the soft-shells of the continental United States. Some are fairly small (10 inches), some are relatively large (20+ inches). Representatives of two of the three species are found in the American west. Those found are one race of the smooth soft-shell and two races of the spiny soft-shell (one of which was introduced to California). The smooth soft-shell is relatively mild-mannered and will usually not attempt to bite if it is gently handled. The spiny soft-shells, however, will bite readily and a bite by an adult can be very painful. All soft-shells have sharp claws, strong legs, and will kick and scratch if given an opportunity.

The smooth and the spiny soft-shells are sexually dimorphic. Males are often only half the size of the adult females.

19. Midland Smooth Soft-shelled Turtle

Apalone mutica mutica

Abundance/Range: The midland smooth soft-shelled turtle is a common but seldom seen turtle. It ranges northward from southeastern Texas to south central South Dakota and eastward to Pennsylvania. In our area it occurs only in central eastern New Mexico.

Habitat: This turtle is most common in rivers with moderate currents and where extensive, open sandbars occur.

Size: Females of this soft-shelled turtle reach slightly more than 12 inches in carapace length; the much smaller males are adult at 4–6 inches. Hatchlings have a carapace length of about 1¼ inches.

Identifying features: The juveniles and males of this softshell have a carapacial ground color of olive tan, light olive brown, or orangish brown. The carapace is patterned with a variable number of small black dots and dashes and is edged with a lighter marginal color that is bordered on the inside with a single black line. The color atop the head, neck, limbs, and tail is similar to that of the carapace. The upper surface of the limbs may be streaked with dark pigment (especially near the apices), but often is not, and the top of the neck may be peppered with fine black dots. The top of the head usually lacks black markings. The undersides of the head, neck, tail, and limbs are cream, yellow(ish), or light tan. A dark-bordered light diagonal line extends downward from the posterior orbit to the neck. A poorly defined light and dark marking, extending onto the snout, is usually present ante-

Midland smooth soft-shelled turtle

rior to each eye. The plastron is usually lighter in color than the brownish underside of the carapace and may be white or gray. The anterior edge of the carapace lacks bumps and spines, and there is no horizontal ridge on the nasal septum (do keep in mind that if you are close enough to any large soft-shell to determine this latter, you are probably close enough to be bitten!).

The entire dorsal surface of adult female smooth soft-shells darkens and assumes a variable blotchy pattern on an olive brown to olive slate ground color.

Belying their actual hardiness, the hatchlings of the smooth soft-shelled turtle are of delicate, almost translucent appearance. The anterior edge of the carapace may fold down and in when the head is withdrawn, and the ribs may often be seen in outline.

Similar species: The various spiny soft-shells have either tubercles or spines on the anterior edge of the carapace and a horizontal ridge on the nasal septum.

ADDITIONAL SUBSPECIES

None within the range of this guide.

20. Texas Spiny Soft-shelled Turtle

Apalone spinifera emoryi

Abundance/Range: Within the range of this guide, the Texas soft-shell is found in restricted areas of Utah, New Mexico, Arizona, southeastern California. It is also found south of the international boundary in northern Mexico.

Habitat: This is primarily a riverine species, but it may also occur in lakes and large ponds.

Size: Like most other soft-shells, the Texas spiny is dimorphic. Females commonly attain a carapace length of 10–15 inches and occasionally grow to 16

■ Texas Spiny Soft-shell
  Apalone spinifera emoryi

■ Western Spiny Soft-shell
  Apalone s. hartwegi

Texas spiny soft-shelled turtle

inches. Adult males are about half that size. Hatchlings are 1¼ inches long.

Identifying features: Dichromatism (sexual differences in color) exists. The carapacial color of males and young females of the Texas spiny soft-shell is tan to olive brown. There are usually tiny white spots on the rear one-third of the carapace. These may or may not be (partially) encircled with dark pigment. The light carapacial marginal band is much wider posteriorly than along the sides and is often edged inside with a single dark line. This is often edged inside with a single dark line. Aged females lose the white spots, the contrast between the marginal marking and the ground color lessens, and their carapace darkens and becomes blotchy. The underside of the carapace, tail, limbs, neck, and chin is white or cream. The dark-edged light ocular stripe is present, but may fragment on the cheek. The feet are spotted distally and the legs streaked at the apices. The top of the head and neck may bear tiny black flecks. A horizontal ridge is present on the nasal septum. The anterior of the carapace bears some conical spines and has a sandpapery texture anteriorly.

Similar species: The carapace of the midland smooth soft-shell lacks the sandpapery texture and the anterior spines. Additionally, the smooth soft-shell lacks horizontal ridges on the nasal septum.

Four additional subspecies occur in the eastern and central states. Only one other, the western spiny soft-shell, occurs in our area of coverage.

ADDITIONAL SUBSPECIES

21. The Western Spiny Soft-shelled Turtle, *Apalone spinifera hartwegi*, lacks white carapacial dots, but has *small* black carapacial spots or flecks. The light carapacial band is usually strongly in evidence and bordered on the inside by a thin black line. The typical dark-edged light facial markings are prominent and the forelimbs are streaked with black. In general, this race is darker in color, and has smaller dark carapacial markings than the other subspecies. Old females, which can attain an 18-inch carapace length, are usually blotched or mottled and lack most if not all contrasting markings. Males are smaller (seldom more than 7 inches long) and may retain some of the juvenile pattern. This soft-shell ranges from Arkansas and Minnesota westward to northeastern New Mexico and Montana.

Western spiny soft-shelled turtle

ASIATIC SOFT-SHELLED TURTLES, GENERA *PALEA* AND *PELODISCUS*

The two species of soft-shells now seen on the Hawaiian Islands are both of Chinese and Vietnamese origin. Both are thought to have been introduced to the islands as a food source in the mid-1800s. They are predominantly aquatic, and considerable numbers may be present in a body of water, yet be overlooked. As soft-shells go, these are both medium-sized species. Because they are covered by fleshy lips, the fact that the mandibles are sharp and strong is not apparent. They are! And the long neck can bring the jaws into contact with a prying hand a fair distance away. Handle large examples with care, and only by the back of the shell. The claws are sharp and the legs are powerful. Avoid these also.

22. Wattle-necked Soft-shelled Turtle

Palea steindachneri

Abundance/Range: It is thought that this turtle was introduced to the Hawaiian Islands in the mid-1800s. It is now established and is relatively common on the Hawaiian Islands of Oahu and Kauai. It is indigenous to China and Vietnam.

Habitat: This soft-shell may be seen in both standing and flowing waters. It inhabits many of the ponds, ditches, canals, marshes, and streams on Oahu and Kauai.

Size: The adult size of this species is 10–16 inches in length. Hatchlings are about 1¼ inches long.

Identifying features: Adults have a dark olive gray, gray, or blackish gray carapace and a light gray plastron with 4 rather poorly defined callosities. The head, limbs, and tail are colored similarly. The carapace is much longer than wide. The name is derived from the cluster of tubercles at the juncture of the carapace and the neck. The neck is very long, the mandibles are sharp, and a large specimen can deliver a long-remembered bite. Horizontal ridges are present on the nasal septum. Hatchlings have an olive brown carapace with well-defined dark brown spots and many rows of tiny tubercles. The plastron is yellowish. The head and neck are olive

Wattle-necked soft-shelled turtle, adult. Photo by Sean McKeown

Wattle-necked soft-shelled turtle, juvenile. Photo by Sean McKeown

brown and there is a pair of large, rearward directed, off-white blotches beginning on the rear of the head and continuing far onto the sides of the neck.

Similar species: The Chinese soft-shelled turtle is the only other species in Hawaii. It is olive green to olive brown and lacks the tubercles on the neck. Hatchlings have a coral red plastron and lack the light patches on the neck.

None.

23. Chinese Soft-shelled Turtle

Pelodiscus sinensis

Abundance/Range: This introduced soft-shelled species is commonly found on the Hawaiian Islands of Oahu and Kauai. It is native to southeastern China and Vietnam. Besides the Hawaiian Islands, it has been introduced to Timor and Japan.

Habitat: This soft-shell is a denizen of drainage ditches, ponds, and slow streams.

Size: At an adult size of 7–10 inches, this is the smaller of the two soft-shells on Hawaii. Hatchlings are about 1¼ inches long.

Identifying features: Adults have a dark olive gray, olive green to olive brown carapace. The elongately oval carapace is somewhat narrower at the front. There are no tubercles lining the front of the carapace. The plas-

Chinese soft-shelled turtle

tron is whitish and bears 7 callosities. The head, limbs, and tail are colored similarly to the carapace. There may be a peppering of tiny black spots on the head and neck. Hatchlings have yellow to coral red plastrons.

Similar species: The wattle-necked soft-shelled turtle is the only other species in Hawaii. It is dark olive gray, olive green, or olive brown and has a row of tubercles along the front of the carapace. Hatchling wattle-necked soft-shells have prominent light patches on the neck.

ADDITIONAL SUBSPECIES

None.

Lizards

Suborder Sauria (Lacertilia)

Worldwide, the suborder Sauria contains more than 3,800 species that are distributed in all but the Antarctic regions. Diverse in habitats, habits, and appearance, these creatures are contained in 400 genera in 24+ families.

All have scales, most have functional limbs with clawed feet (but some are legless), and most have functional eyes with lids. Others have functional eyes protected by a transparent, spectacle-like brille rather than by lids, and yet others lack functional eyes. The tails of lizards as a group may be short and broad, short and slender, or long and tapered. Many lizards have tails that break (autotomize) if stressed, and some do so with rather remarkable ease. To facilitate breakage, the tail (caudal) vertebrae may possess fracture planes—weakened areas in the bone.

Lizards vary in size from the massive girth and 9-foot length of the Komodo dragon to the soda-straw thickness of some 1½-inch geckos.

Lizards are very well represented in western North America, and although none are native, 20 species have been introduced to Hawaii.

Within these pages we will discuss 11 families that contain 106 species and a total of 144 recognized subspecies.

These are categorized as follows:

- Alligator Lizards, family Anguidae (4 species)
- Legless Lizards, family Anniellidae (1 species)
- Chameleons, family Chamaeleonidae (2 species)
- Eyelidded Geckos, family Eublepharidae (3 species)
- Typical Geckos, family Gekkonidae (11 species)
- Gila Monster, family Helodermatidae (1 species)
- Iguanas, family Iguanidae and relatives, Iguanas (48 species)
- Old World Lizards, family Lacertidae (1 species)
- Skinks, family Scincidae (9 species)
- Whiptails and Racerunners, family Teiidae (20 species)
- Night Lizards, family Xantusiidae (6 species)

Most of our native lizards are of very typical overall appearance (long bodied, four legs, and a long tail), but a few types, such as the legless lizards, chameleons, and Gila monster, diverge from the norm. Although most of our lizards have ear openings, a few species do not. Some have legs so short that they are hardly noticeable, and one species lacks legs entirely. The various horned lizards look like animated pincushions. Most lizards are diurnal to crepuscular in their activity patterns, but many of the geckos are primarily nocturnal.

Most lizards are terrestrial, but a few colonize trees or dwellings. Although a few species are associated with the edges of waterways, no lizard within the range of this book is truly aquatic.

The Gila monster is dangerously venomous, the only lizard of the United States to be so.

9

Alligator Lizards

Family Anguidae

Although in the east this lizard family includes the glass lizards, the family Anguidae is represented in the American west only by four species of alligator lizards. Morphological differences in the species are minimal, and it may be necessary to have the lizard in hand to check eye color to assure accurate identification. It is even more difficult to differentiate the subspecies within a species. In some cases range can be as positive an identifier as appearance. Three of the four species are rather well known; the fourth, the Panamint alligator lizard, is a comparative rarity.

Reproduction may be by oviparity (southern, Arizona, and Panamint alligator lizards) or ovoviviparity (northern alligator lizards). Females may provide care for the eggs throughout the incubation period or for live babies for a much shorter time period.

These lizards have a longitudinal lateral expansion fold from beneath the tympanum to the rear leg. This allows a degree of expansion after eating or when the female is gravid. Because they have osteoderms (bony plates beneath each epidermal scale) the alligator lizards lack some of the sinuosity displayed by other elongate lizards and the snakes. Eyelids and ear openings are present.

The legs of the alligator lizards are short but fully functional. However, when startled, the lizards usually fold the legs against the body and glide forward by means of lateral undulations.

All of our anguids have proportionately long tails. The alligator lizards have caudal fracture planes (a weakened area in a caudal vertebra to facilitate ready breakage). The tail regenerates well and almost fully, yet has a scalation different from the original.

Montane Yellows

I had been scanning a few of the reptile-related forums when a photograph posted by "J.P." caught my eye. It was of a Sierra alligator lizard, *Elgaria coerulea palmeri*. But unlike the greenish examples of this subspecies with which I was familiar, the one pictured was a definite and beautiful yellow.

I tracked down J.P., who resided in northern central California, and asked him whether it would be possible to see one of these pretty lizards on my next trip to California. He felt that it would, so a few months later, on a balmy spring day, I hopped in the car and headed again from Florida to California.

Three days and many dollars worth of gasoline later, two friends plus J.P. and I were on a narrow paved road winding upward through montane conifers into the Sierras of northern California.

That day J.P. took us to areas where long-fallen spruce and firs were lying like matchsticks, bark shards peeling in huge plates. Woodpeckers hammered and chortled overhead. Juncos exploded from cover at our feet. That the hodgepodge of fallen, moldering trunks was perfect cover for alligator lizards was reflected by the fact that Sierra alligator lizards were everywhere. But there were no yellow ones. So we moved on to some nearly pristine boggy mountain meadows through which narrow crystal clear streams bubbled over rocky bottoms. Beneath the natural cover were more Sierra alligator lizards. Some were *almost* yellow, but none came close in color intensity to those in J.P.'s photos. We drove and traipsed from site to site, but in the end we failed and had to call it a day without finding one.

Maybe it was the time of year. Perhaps the bright yellow is assumed only by dominant males in breeding readiness. Perhaps we simply failed to find a yellow one. But despite the whys and wherefores of this failure, we were fortunate enough to have seen magnificent montane vistas in settings that had to be seen to be believed; to walk amid towering trees on craggy mountains, and to learn in the most graphic sense that there are regions and habitats still unknown to me.

WESTERN ALLIGATOR LIZARDS, GENUS *ELGARIA*

These lizards are primarily insectivorous, but may occasionally eat small vertebrates.

Female southern alligator lizards produce up to 41 eggs, but most clutches contain between 8 and 20 eggs; 6–12 eggs seems the norm for the Arizona alligator lizard. Not too surprisingly, larger females have the largest clutches. Northern alligator lizards have up to 15 live babies. Other than the fact that they are oviparous, the reproductive biology of the Panamint alligator lizard is virtually unknown.

Gravid females preferentially choose an area that will hold at least a small amount of ground moisture for deposition. A site beneath a fallen trunk or a flat rock may prove ideal.

If threatened the alligator lizard will inflate its body (distending the lateral groove), and gape the jaws. The bite is strong but not dangerous. These lizards may be encountered as they cross trails in the morning, bask in the rays of the lowering sun amid rocks near canyon springs in the late afternoon, or lie quietly concealed beneath surface cover.

Northern Alligator Lizards, *Elgaria coerulea* ssp.

These lizards have from 14 scale rows (northwestern alligator lizard) to 16 scale rows (all others) of platelike scales across the back. Although these are usually the least colorful of the four species of western alligator lizard, individuals in some populations become suffused with a striking yellow overlay during the breeding season. Dark crossbands, if present, are irregular and often incomplete. Although they may have some flecks of yellow in their eyes, the various subspecies of this elongate lizard all have primarily dark eyes. This will at least differentiate them from the yellow-eyed southern alligator lizards. Dorsal, lateral, and limb scales are keeled. Use range to identify subspecies.

24. San Francisco Alligator Lizard

Elgaria coerulea coerulea

Abundance/Range: This secretive but common lizard has a small range in central coastal California to the north, south, and east of San Francisco Bay, California.

Habitat: This lizard may be found in habitats as diverse as damp woodlands and semiarid desert scrub. It may be found beneath tidal wrack as well as far inland under fallen logs, rocks and artificial cover. The various subspecies are found from sea level to at least 10,500 feet in elevation.

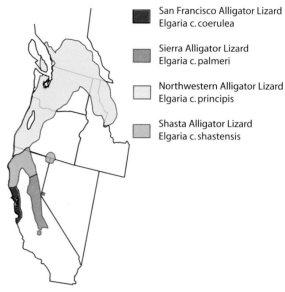

San Francisco Alligator Lizard
Elgaria c. coerulea

Sierra Alligator Lizard
Elgaria c. palmeri

Northwestern Alligator Lizard
Elgaria c. principis

Shasta Alligator Lizard
Elgaria c. shastensis

San Francisco alligator lizard

Size: Adults are 11–12½ inches in total length. The tail of this slender lizard is about twice the length of its head and body. Neonates are about 3½ inches long.

Identifying features: This lizard is an olive brown, olive gray, slate gray, or tan above with dark dorsal blotches, and short, vertical black bars edged posteriorly with white, on the sides. Neonates are often a beautiful metallic olive gold dorsally. The temporal (cheek) scales are keeled. The belly is gray(ish). A dark longitudinal stripe edges each scale. Dorsal scales may be in 14–16 rows. The lateral groove is well developed and graphically separates the dorsum from the venter. The scales in the groove are very tiny and granular. The head is lance shaped and covered dorsally and laterally with prominent overlapping scales. All four legs are well developed, but appear proportionately short.

Similar species: The southern alligator lizard has yellow eyes and the dark lines are in the center of each belly scale. Skinks are shiny, have smooth, unkeeled scales, and lack a lateral groove.

Comments: When in the open, the San Francisco alligator lizard is alert and moves quietly to safety as a disturbance nears. It can climb well, and uses its tail to steady itself. The tail is strong and prehensile enough to easily support the entire weight of the lizard, yet it autotomizes easily.

ADDITIONAL SUBSPECIES

25. The Sierra Alligator Lizard, *Elgaria coerulea palmeri*, is found throughout the Sierra Nevada Mountains of central California. The temporal scales are keeled. Scales are in 16 rows across the back. Dorsal markings may be complete bands, partial bands, or virtually absent.

Sierra alligator lizard

Northwestern alligator lizard

26. Northwestern Alligator Lizard, *Elgaria coerulea principis*, has the most northerly distribution of any member of this family in North America. It is found from southern British Columbia southward to southeastern Oregon. This subspecies has the dorsal scales in 14 rows. The back coloration is often in the form of a broad tan to gray stripe that contrasts with the sides in color. This is a small subspecies.

27. Shasta Alligator Lizard, *Elgaria coerulea shastensis*, has a spotty distribution in northwestern Nevada and adjacent Oregon and a larger, seem-

Shasta alligator lizard

ingly continuous range, from southwestern Oregon to northwestern California. The temporal scales are smooth (not keeled). Scales are in 16 rows across the back.

Southern Alligator Lizards, *Elgaria multicarinata* ssp.

The scales across the back are keeled and in 14 rows. A dark longitudinal line is present in the center of each ventral scale. The three subspecies of southern alligator lizard have yellow irises. Crossbands are more regular than on the northern alligator lizards. The crossbands are often black edged with white on the sides and reddish on the back.

28. California Alligator Lizard

Elgaria multicarinata multicarinata

Abundance/Range: A common lizard, this race occurs from northern to central California and on the Channel Islands.

Habitat: These lizards are found from mountain fastnesses to suburban backyards. They may be found from sea level to habitats at more than 5,000 feet in elevation.

Size: This is the largest of the western alligator lizards. Although most adults are between 9 and 12 inches in length, a few have been authenticated at more than 16 inches long. Hatchlings are about 3½ inches long.

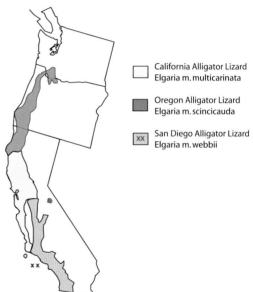

California Alligator Lizard
Elgaria m. multicarinata

Oregon Alligator Lizard
Elgaria m. scincicauda

San Diego Alligator Lizard
Elgaria m. webbii

Identifying features: This is a very elongate, long-tailed lizard. The ground color is variable. It may be gray, brown, olive brown, or reddish. There are red blotches on the back. The top of the head is mottled. The dorsal scales are weakly keeled. The temporal scales are weakly keeled. Hatchlings may have a gold, olive, or brown back with no prominent markings.

Similar species: The various subspecies of the northern alligator lizard have dark eyes and the belly-scale striping is between the scales rather than on the center of each.

California alligator lizard

Comment: The differences in the three subspecies of the southern alligator lizard are very subtle. Rely on range to assist with subspecific identifications.

ADDITIONAL SUBSPECIES

29. The Oregon Alligator Lizard, *Elgaria multicarinata scincicauda*, ranges southward from central Washington to northwestern California. This subspecies tends to be less colorful than the others, but some individuals are very brightly marked. There is no mottling on the top of the head. The temporal scales are only weakly keeled. The dorsal scales are also weakly keeled.

Oregon alligator lizard

San Diego alligator lizard

30. The San Diego Alligator Lizard, *Elgaria multicarinata webbii*, ranges from the northern Sierra Nevada Range of central California southward to central western Baja California. This, the most robust and heavily keeled of the races, lacks mottling on the top of the head. The many crossbars are prominent and usually multicolored. The bars on the sides are black edged posteriorly with white, and the bars on the back consist of red, black, and white scales.

Arizona and Panamint Alligator Lizards

31. Arizona Alligator Lizard

Elgaria kingii nobilis

Abundance/Range: This fairly common lizard ranges southward from central Arizona and southwestern New Mexico to central western Sonora and adjacent Chihuahua, Mexico.

Habitat: This montane lizard may be found in coniferous forests, in scrub and chaparral, and in grassy, rock-strewn woodland openings. It is commonly encountered in debris at the foot of talus slopes, and beneath cover in campsites and parking lot edges. Its elevational parameters are from about 2,000 feet to about 9,000 feet.

Arizona alligator lizard

Size: Adults range from 8 to 12½ inches in length. Tail is about 250% of the snout-vent length. Hatchlings are about 3 inches in length.

Identifying features: This pretty lizard has dark brown, reddish brown, or olive brown bands against a tan, pinkish, or gray ground color. There is a black and white pattern on the lips. The scales are in 14 rows and are smooth or only weakly keeled. The belly is light with dark spots. Hatchlings are patterned like the adults but are more strongly colored and precisely banded.

Similar species: None within the range of this lizard.

Comment: Together with its Mexican subspecies, this lizard is referred to as the Madrean alligator lizard.

ADDITIONAL SUBSPECIES

There are Mexican subspecies.

32. Panamint Alligator Lizard

Elgaria panamintina

Abundance/Range: Perhaps because of its remote range, this alligator lizard seems more uncommon than it actually is. Populations are locally distributed in the Inyo, Panamint, and White mountains of central western California.

Habitat: This montane lizard may be found in coniferous forests, in scrub and chaparral, and in grassy, rock-strewn woodland openings and in canyons. It is occasionally seen near talus slopes. It seems most common amid the brush and rocks near desert springs. It occurs from 2,800 to more than 7,500 feet in elevation.

Size: Adults range from 8 to 12½ inches in length. Tail is about 250% of the snout-vent length. Hatchlings are about 3 inches in length.

Identifying features: This pretty lizard has broad, dark brown, reddish brown, or olive brown bands against a tan, yellowish, or pinkish ground color. The lips are unmarked. The scales are in 14 rows and are smooth or only weakly keeled. The belly may be light with scattered smudges, or there may be a narrow, dark, longitudinal stripe on the center of each scale. Hatchlings are patterned like the adults but are more strongly colored and precisely banded.

Similar species: None within the range of this lizard.

ADDITIONAL SUBSPECIES

None.

Panamint alligator lizard

10

Legless Lizards

Family Anniellidae

There are only two species in this lizard family, *Anniella pulchra*, discussed here, and *A. geronimensis*, from coastal northern Baja. Both are persistent burrowers and both often dwell in the almost perpetually cool oceanside spray zone.

These are small lizards with an attenuate body and a rather short tail that autotomizes readily.

The eyes are reduced in size but retain functional lids. The snout is wedge shaped and the lower jaw is countersunk, both adaptations for the lizard's success as a burrower.

Legless lizards are ovoviviparous, giving birth to 1–4 (normally 2 or 3) live young each autumn.

The lizards are predominantly insectivorous, eating burrowing insects and their larvae; however, spiders are also occasionally eaten.

Although legless lizards are often encountered in the very dry surface layers, they desiccate quickly if denied access to moist soil at deeper levels.

The Legless Ones

Robert Sprackland had said that all I needed to do to see a black-phase legless lizard (*Anniella pulchra*) would be to visit him in the Monterey Bay (California) area and he would show me one.

So I did just that, and he certainly made good on his promise. Robert not only showed me the creatures in the wild, but also introduced me to a researcher who was keeping several hundred of the creatures destined for reintroduction after completion of a construction project in their habitat.

Finding a few in the wild was the best part of the visit, though. Robert took me to some rolling dunes overlooking the Pacific Ocean, and under the sand beneath the dunes vegetation we soon found several of the pencil-sized insectivores.

Legless lizards, no matter their color phase, are interesting little creatures. They are persistent, obligatory burrowers with narrowed eyes and a tail that autotomizes with very little encouragement from any outside source. They feed upon tiny burrowing arthropods and annelids.

It was in a San Diego backyard, rather than at a picturesque seashore locale, that Brad Smith and I found a large legless lizard of the silvery phase. We found the lizard beneath the duff under an Australian pine. It was a beautifully colored creature that did not even seem too disturbed by being uncovered.

With the silvery and the black phases now found, it is time to seek out the intermediate phase, a dusky-colored creature that occurs in the area of Morro Bay, California. It is always good to have a goal and very satisfying to fulfill that goal.

33. California Legless Lizard

Anniella pulchra

Abundance/Range: The population statistics of this lizard are poorly known. Despite an extensive range, it is of spotty distribution, and many historic populations have been extirpated by development. Yet the lizard continues to be relatively abundant in other areas. Because of its burrowing habits it is seldom seen even where common. It ranges northward from northern Baja California to the vicinity of San Francisco Bay, California.

Silvery Legless Lizard
Anniella pulchra

xx Black color phase

xx Dusky color morph

Habitat: This burrowing lizard may be found in seaside dunes, sandy backyards, city parks, and other areas having sandy substrates or an inch or two of decomposed leaf litter (duff). It is found from sea level to elevations of about 5,000 feet. It is most often found beneath flowering plants and shrubs.

Size: This lizard is adult at 6 to about 10½ inches in total length. The tail length is considerably shorter than the snout-vent length. Neonates are 3¼ inches long.

Identifying features: This is the only legless lizard in the American west. There are none in Canada. The legless lizard is restricted in distribution to California. Both body and tail are cylindrical. The tail is blunt tipped and barely tapers.

There are three color classes, but subspecies are not currently recognized.

33a. Silvery phase: The dorsum is silvery tan and the belly is bright yellow, olive yellow, or occasionally gray. There is a prominent black vertebral stripe. Two very thin black stripes separate the dorsal color from the ventral color. This phase is found over the entire range except as noted below.

33b. Black phase: When adult this phase is brownish black to charcoal above, lemon yellow to olive yellow below. Stripes are largely obscured by the dark dorsal color. Juveniles are lighter in overall color than the adults and the stripes are prominent. This phase is found in the vicinity of Monterey Bay, California.

33c. Dusky phase: Brown above and variably yellow below. The dark dorsal color often obscures the vertebral and lateral stripes. This is the predominant phase in the vicinity of Morro Bay, California.

The neonates of all three color forms are similar to the silvery phase in

California legless lizard, silvery phase

California legless lizard, black phase

color. The overlying dark coloration is assumed with increasing size and advancing age.

Similar species: None.

Comment: Although the dusky phase of the legless lizard was never designated as a subspecies, the silvery and the black forms were long considered subspecifically distinct. You will find the silvery form listed in many publications as *Anniella pulchra pulchra* and the black form as *Anniella pulchra nigra*.

A silvery phase that differs genetically from those surrounding it has recently been found in the vicinity of Bakersfield, California. It has not yet (late 2008) been formally described.

ADDITIONAL SUBSPECIES

Currently none.

California legless lizard, dusky phase

11

True Chameleons

Family Chamaeleonidae

The true chameleons are of Old World distribution. However, the yellow-crested Jackson's chameleon, a popular pet species, has been established in the Hawaiian Islands since 1972 and is now known from the vicinity of Morro Bay, California as well. More recently the veiled chameleon has been found on the Hawaiian island of Maui as well as in a residential Los Angeles neighborhood. This is another very popular pet species.

At nearly a foot in length, male Jackson's chameleons are larger than females, and adorned with three facial horns. Lacking horns, the veiled chameleon instead has a proportionately immense casque atop its head.

Chameleons have clasping (tonglike) toes on each foot and a strongly prehensile tail that does not autotomize. They are laterally flattened, and this species bears a serrate vertebral crest. The eyes are protuberant and capable of independent motion, allowing a chameleon to look directly behind it with one eye while looking straight forward with the other. The tongue is long and protrusible and has a sticky, grasping tip with which a chameleon is able to capture insects several inches distant. When the lizard is stalking an insect, both eyes are directed forward, providing the lizard binocular vision by which to accurately assess distance.

Chameleons move slowly, often in stilted fashion, through the trees. They often stop and wave slowly back and forth like a breeze-fluttered leaf.

Color changes are more influenced by stress (including surrounding temperature, body temperature, territorial sparring, and health) than by background. Various greens, yellows, tans, pale blues, browns, grays, and black may be assumed.

Chameleons are very territorial. Males joust each other with the horns and may actually bite each other when two or more are close. The mere sighting of a distant male will alter the activity pattern and body color of a second male.

Jackson's chameleon gives live birth. Up to 50 babies may be produced annually in a single litter, but the more normal number is 10–25. The veiled chameleon is oviparous and very fecund. Several clutches of up to 50 eggs each may be produced annually.

The Sticky-tongued Ones

The tiny lizard stood gently swaying on a twig-tip of a low shrub in Ft. Myers, Florida. Its tail was in a watchspring coil and its turreted, independently moving eyes searched the surroundings for insect prey or for predator. The former would be caught on the tip of a projectable tongue that is nearly as long as the head and body length of the lizard; chameleons depend on camouflage to protect them from the latter. The bundled toes of the lizard gripped the twig so tightly that it would be difficult to remove the lizard if I chose to try.

This was the first place in the United States that this popular pet lizard, the veiled chameleon, *Chamaeleo c. calyptratus*, was known to be established. A native of Yemen, it has since been found in several other southern Florida locales and more recently in California.

I looked more carefully at the little lizard. Heel spurs (calcars) indicated that the baby, then barely 3 inches long, was a male. But at that stage in its life, although the calcars indicated its gender, there was nothing at

continued

all to hint that this was one of the largest of the chameleon species and that when adult it could be 24 inches in overall length (females are much smaller).

Although this was the first veiled chameleon I had seen in the wild, I had encountered another species, the yellow-crested Jackson's chameleon, a strange appearing creature with three prominent facial horns, in Brandon, Florida, more than thirty years earlier. There I had rented a house having a large yard and a pasture. Although there was no livestock, several strands of barbed wire, stretched tightly from fence post to fence post around the several-acre pasture, proclaimed that if livestock had been within it would have remained there.

To my amazement, as I drove from the property one morning, a big male yellow-crested Jackson's chameleon, *Chamaeleo jacksonii xantholophus*, a lizard of African origin, was thermoregulating on one of those strands of barbed wire. Where, I wondered, had that come from? And once I was aware of its presence and had developed a search image, I found that there were many, many others. Males, females, and neonates were present. I was never quite sure of the origin of those chameleons, but even then they were a popular pet trade species and the property owner from whom we rented not only knew what they were, but protected them rigorously from collectors.

But things change. Over the years that once rural area has been developed. Where once stood the "chameleon pasture" there are now condominiums. The chameleon colony is long gone.

Though seemingly gone from Florida, however, this 15-inch-long chameleon species remains a component of the herpetofauna of the United States. It is firmly established on several of the Hawaiian Islands and has been more recently found in California in the vicinity of Morro Bay and Laguna Beach. And although it doesn't belong here, as the most unique appearing lizard of the United States, Jackson's chameleons have a place in the hearts of most observers. It seems likely that these lizards, unique in appearance and habits, will continue to persist.

34. Yellow-crested (Mt. Kenya) Jackson's Chameleon

Chamaeleo jacksonii xantholophus

Abundance/Range: Indigenous to the vicinity of Mt. Kenya in East Africa, this species is relatively common in Hawaii (present on all of the main islands except Molokai), where it has been established for at least two decades. It is also tenuously established in the vicinity of Morro Bay, California.

Habitat: This is an exclusively arboreal lizard. Adults may be found in shade trees and large shrubs. Juveniles tend to remain closer to the ground in low shrubs and even on herbaceous plants (such as garden flower and vegetable plants).

Size: This is a large lizard that is noticeably compressed from side to side. It is adult at about 12 inches in length. Neonates are about 1¾ inches long.

Identifying features: Adult examples of this chameleon are usually of some shade of green. Although best known for its color changing ability,

Yellow-crested Jackson's chameleon, male

Yellow-crested Jackson's chameleon, female

the secondary adaptations of this lizard are equally notable. Chameleons have the following characteristics:

- bundled toes on each foot (2 on the outside and 3 on the inside of the forefeet and 3 on the outside and 2 on the inside of the rear feet
- strongly prehensile tail used like a fifth hand, or may be tightly coiled like a watch spring
- laterally flattened body
- horns; adult males have 3 facial horns; adult females have mere nubbins in place of the horns
- a strongly serrate vertebral crest

Hatchlings tend to be brown with white dashes on the upper sides. **Similar species:** See account 35a for the veiled chameleon.

ADDITIONAL SUBSPECIES

None in the United States.

35. Veiled Chameleon

Chamaeleo calyptratus calyptratus

Abundance/Range: This chameleon, native to Yemen, has been reported from near the city of Los Angeles, California. It is also currently (2006) established on Maui, Hawaii, where efforts are now underway to eradicate it.

Habitat: Adults are found in shade trees and large shrubs; neonates are usually closer to the ground.

Size: Males attain a length of nearly 24 inches; females are only 14 inches long. Hatchlings are about 2¼ inches long.

Identifying features: Turquoise and gold, turquoise and white, or green are all commonly assumed colors. Males have a huge (occasionally to 4 inches in height) cranial crest (casque). Females have a proportionately lower casque. The body is laterally flattened and a vertebral crest is present. Hatchlings are green with a few white or purplish spots on the sides. Males of all ages have a spur (calcar) on each heel.

Similar species: The yellow-crested Jackson's chameleon lacks a high casque and males have three facial horns. At present, the ranges of the Jackson's and the veiled chameleons are not known to overlap.

Veiled chameleon, male

Comments: This amazingly fecund chameleon can attain sexual maturity at 6 months of age, lay up to 70 eggs in a clutch, and produce several clutches annually.

ADDITIONAL SUBSPECIES

None in North America.

12

Eyelidded Geckos

Family Eublepharidae

This is a small family of lizards that is represented in the New World by only a single genus, *Coleonyx*. Because of a rather standardized body pattern, these small, delicate appearing lizards are often referred to colloquially as banded geckos. The New World representatives are terrestrial and nocturnal, have functional eyelids, and lack  expanded toepads. All have vertically elliptical pupils. Males have prominent anal spurs and pheromone-releasing preanal pores. These pores are arranged in a V, anterior to the vent.

Tail (caudal) scalation is arranged in rings.

All of these geckos are insectivores, and all are oviparous. A female annually lays several clutches of 2 eggs each.

When moving rapidly or when hunting, eublepharines will raise and writhe the tail. The tail is easily autotomized (broken free), but quickly regenerates. Regenerated tails have scaling noticeably different from the original.

BANDED GECKOS, GENUS *COLEONYX*

Of the three species of banded gecko in the American west (none occur in Canada or Hawaii), two, the Texas Banded gecko and the western desert banded gecko, are of wide distribution and are well known. The third, Switak's banded gecko, is of restricted distribution in the United States and is protected.

Age-related pattern and color changes are marked. Young examples are strikingly banded in blacks and yellows. With growth and age the pattern becomes more diffuse, with dark pigment encroaching on light and vice versa. Old adults of all species in this group may be reticulate rather than banded.

Seen in the glow of car headlights as they dart across the road like diminutive, low-slung mice, most eublepharines appear silvery.

Inexplicably and erroneously, some persons believe these innocuous geckos to be venomous!

Found! A Western Rarity

Two common species of eublepharine gecko are found in the United States (none in Canada), plus two less frequently seen species. Because of my poor timing, it had taken me years of looking to find a reticulated gecko in West Texas. I was beginning to think a similar time frame would occur on my search for Switak's banded gecko, *Coleonyx switaki*, in southern California. The problem probably wasn't that the lizards were rare or even uncommon, but rather that my visits didn't seem to coincide with the humid spring and summer nights when the species was active.

But finally, more by accident than intent, I was in the range of this gecko on a hot, humid, summer night. I drove a dozen or more times up and down the stretch of road on which they seem to occur most frequently. Finally tiring of seeing (imagining, actually—the night was too dark to see) the same cliffs and boulder fields time and again, I decided to change venue and took a quick ride through the low and very hot desert. It was a revitalizing side trip. Sidewinders, glossy snakes, and shovel-nosed snakes were still active, and desert banded geckos were abundant.

At 3:00 A.M. I decided to make one last run through the mountains. Why not? It was on the way back to the motel anyway. A speckled rattlesnake was crossing. A night snake moved quickly across the pavement. A lyre snake and desert banded geckos were on the side of the road. Twists, turns, horseshoe curves, a straightaway—a silvery lizard in the headlight's glow! I stopped quickly, hopped from the car, and did a little celebratory dance on the roadside! That lizard seen at 3:17 A.M.—that little silvery appearing lizard—was the much desired Switak's banded gecko.

36. Texas Banded Gecko

Coleonyx brevis

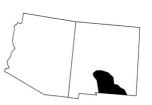

Abundance/Range: This is a common gecko that occurs widely in southern and western Texas. It is also known from southeastern New Mexico and is widely distributed in northeastern Mexico.

Habitat: The Texas banded gecko favors semiarid to arid natural areas with ample ground cover. It is particularly common in areas where flat rocks and succulent vegetative debris are found. Rocky hillsides, canyonlands, and creviced escarpments are typical habitats. It may also be found near human habitations, where it seeks seclusion beneath boards, discarded roofing tins, and other such human-generated debris. This species may be found at elevations between sea level and 5,000 feet.

Size: This is the smallest eublepharine in the United States. Texas banded geckos are adult at 3½–4 inches in total length and can reach a maximum size of 4⅞ inches. The tail is about equal in length to the length of the head and body.

Hatchlings are about 1¾ inches in total length.

Identifying features: The dorsal and lateral scales of this species are nontuberculate.

Hatchling Texas geckos are rather precisely patterned in darker-edged, dark brown and creamy yellow bands of about equal width. With aging, the edges of the bands obscure and become difficult to discern. Light pigment usually appears in the dark fields. Old adults may appear mottled

Texas banded gecko

rather than banded. Black spots occur in both the dark and the light fields. Metachrosis is not marked, but these geckos are often lighter at night than during the day. Texas banded geckos are differentiated from the more westerly *Coleonyx variegatus* ssp. by the arrangement of the preanal pores. The pores of the Texas banded gecko form an incomplete V, the apex being separated at the midline.

Voice: If frightened (including while being restrained) or involved in territoriality disputes, male Texas banded geckos may produce barely audible squeaks.

Similar species: In the western United States the range of this small gecko does not overlap or abut the range of any other eublepharine.

ADDITIONAL SUBSPECIES

None.

37. Desert Banded Gecko

Coleonyx variegatus variegatus

San Diego Banded Gecko
Coleonyx variegatus abbotti

Desert Banded Gecko
Coleonyx v. variegatus

Utah Banded Gecko
Coleonyx variegatus utahensis

Tucson Banded Gecko
Coleonyx variegatus bogerti

Abundance/Range: Because of its nocturnal lifestyle, this abundant gecko is often overlooked. This subspecies ranges widely in southeastern California, western Arizona, and northern sections of the Mexican states of Baja and Sonora.

Habitat: This gecko utilizes many desert and semidesert habitats. It may be found amid rocks, in canyons, on grassy hillsides, on open dunes, and in association with creosote and chaparral. It hides by day in rodent burrows or beneath surface objects.

Size: This gecko is adult at 6 inches in total length, but is usually not more than 4½–5 inches long. The tail is equal to the head and body in length. Hatchlings are almost 2½ inches long.

Identifying features: This is a well-known desert lizard. Hatchlings are prominently banded in brown and yellow or brown and cream, but with age the pattern diffuses somewhat and the dark bands may be represented by numerous spots. The scales are smooth and nontuberculate. The belly is white. Males have 5–7 preanal pores that V at the midline. Adults often have dark spots in the light fields of color.

Voice: As with most other geckos, males of this species are able to produce weak squeaking notes. These are given during times of stress or during territoriality disputes.

Similar species: In extreme south central California, desert banded geckos are sympatric with Switak's banded gecko. The latter may be differentiated by its many scattered tuberculate scales.

Comment: The morphological characteristics of the subspecies of the desert banded gecko are variable and subjective. Additionally, the various subspecies intergrade at the periphery of the ranges, producing offspring with a confusing suite of characteristics. It is difficult to differentiate sub-

Desert banded gecko

Desert banded gecko

species using appearance alone. Rely on range maps to assist you with this chore, and even then be prepared to say, "I don't know."

Collectively, these geckos are also referred to as western geckos.

ADDITIONAL SUBSPECIES

38. The San Diego Banded Gecko, *Coleonyx variegatus abbotti*, ranges southward from Riverside County, California, to the northern portion of Baja California Sur. This is a pretty subspecies with dark bands of the same width or narrower than the light interspaces. The dark bands do not have light centers. The head is unspotted.

Desert banded gecko

San Diego banded gecko

Tucson banded gecko

39. The Tucson Banded Gecko, *Coleonyx variegatus bogerti*, occurs from central southern Arizona and northern Sonora, Mexico to extreme southwestern New Mexico. It differs from the desert banded gecko only in having 8 or more preanal pores.

40. The Utah Banded Gecko, *Coleonyx variegatus utahensis*, occurs in extreme southwestern Utah and northwestern Arizona to southeastern Nevada. The dark bands of this race have uneven edges and are usually wider than the light bands.

Utah banded gecko

41. Switak's Banded Gecko

Coleonyx switaki

Abundance/Range: Because this gecko lives in such a remote area, and mostly within a state park, its population statistics are relatively unknown. Certainly this gecko is infrequently seen, but whether it is rare, secretive, or both has not been ascertained. It is found southward from the vicinity of Borrego Springs in San Diego County, California, to northeastern Baja California Sur. This is a protected species.

Habitat: Canyons, boulder-strewn hillsides, and plots of rock-strewn land in thornscrub deserts are the favored habitats of the Switak's banded gecko. It is occasionally seen at night on paved roads.

Size: This is the largest member of the genus in our area of coverage. Fully grown male Switak's banded geckos may attain 6½ inches in total length. The tail is equal to the head and body in length. Besides being large, this gecko is relatively heavy bodied. Hatchlings are about 3 inches in total length.

Identifying features: Hatchlings of this large and poorly understood gecko may be yellow green to olive in ground coloration and have the light

Switak's banded gecko

bands represented by rows of round spots. Colors dull with growth, but accentuate again when males become reproductively active. Nonbreeding adults have a ground color of pinkish gray to yellow gray to gray, and the crossrows of spots are off-white. The tail is prominently banded in black and off-white. There is a scattering of tuberculate scales on the back and sides.

Voice: As with most other geckos, males of this species are able to produce weak squeaking notes.

Similar species: The various subspecies of the desert banded gecko lack tuberculate scales on the dorsum.

13

Typical Geckos

Family Gekkonidae

Eight of the nine species of typical geckos in the American West and Hawaii are non-natives. All have expanded toepads and lack eyelids. Most species occur in Hawaii.

Seven of these geckos are nocturnal and arboreal and have filled a niche largely unexploited by any of our other lizards. Three species are diurnal and arboreal. Most are closely tied to human habitations where they hunt insects in the glow of porch or street lights. Because of their toepads they can climb even smooth surfaces, including walls and glass, with agility. The toepads are more complex than they might seem. The pads are transversely divided into a series of lamellae that contain vast numbers of tiny bristlelike setae. The setae are tipped with an equally vast number of microscopic, nonskid hairs, and these are again subdivided into millions more. To put it in a most unscientific way, static cling is the force that allows the geckos to climb. To fully appreciate the complexity of these climbing devices, simply watch the way a slowly moving gecko curls its toes upward, from tip inward, when disengaging a foot.

All of these geckos lack functional eyelids, their eyes being protected instead with a clear spectacle (the brille).

All are cold sensitive but, on heated dwellings and warehouses, manage to survive the winter's cold.

All of these typical geckos have a voice. As might be imagined, the vocalizations of the tiny house geckos are mere clicks or squeaks.

All geckos have an easily broken tail. Some species are capable of autotomizing their tail with little, if any, external help. A great many geckos seen in the field have a partially to fully regenerated tail. These always differ in scalation and appearance from the originals.

Male geckos are territorial at all times, but are especially so during the breeding season. Serious skirmishes can occur if two males meet and one does not quickly back down. A gecko's skin is thin and can be easily torn free, often permitting an attacked gecko to escape a predator. A gecko's skin also heals quickly.

Many of these geckos are capable of remarkable color changes. They are darker and (often) more heavily patterned by day, lighter and less contrastingly patterned by night.

Most species lay several clutches of two eggs each, every spring and summer. Some reproduce almost year-round.

Both sexes occur in most of the geckos of the continental United States and Hawaii. However, a few types are all-female, unisexual species and reproduce parthenogenetically. Depending on which of the terms fits best in a sentence, any of the three terms—unisexual, all female, or parthenogenetic—may be used interchangeably in the species discussions.

A Sticky-toed One

It was another of those muggy nights during the dark of the late spring moon and I was back in California. This time it was just a general photography trip, but as always reptiles and amphibians were foremost on my mind. I had decided to try to photograph the varying patterns of several desert banded geckos so I headed for the desert near Borrego Springs. It is an area—just one of many, of course—where banded geckos are truly abundant.

The route I chose to drive took me through some impressive mountains. In these, along the road cuts, it was not unusual to see snakes as diverse as blind snakes, speckled rattlers, and California kings. This night all of these and more were out and active.

But at one point about halfway down the mountain I began noticing tiny, flattened lizards in the road. At first I thought that all were vehicular lizardicides, tiny corpses left by passing traffic. Still I had to know what they were, so I slowed and stopped at the next one. As I stopped it scuttled off toward the rock face that edged the road. It (and all of the others, it proved) was a leaf-toed gecko, *Phyllodactylus nocticolus*, and although a few were road casualties, most seemed to be merely thermoregulating on the still-warm pavement. Although traffic was light, this would assuredly prove fatal to a few more of the little straddle-legged lizards before the night was over.

STUMP-TOED GECKOS, GENUS *GEHYRA*

Within this large genus of geckos are both small and large species. Many of the species are polymorphic. They range throughout Oceania to Asia, and Madagascar. Despite the name, the toes are reasonably long and may have either undivided or divided lamellae beneath. The innermost toe lacks a claw. A single species, the small but stocky *G. mutilata*, occurs on Hawaii.

42. Stump-toed Gecko

Gehyra mutilata

Abundance/Range: This small gecko is known to be present on all of the main Hawaiian Islands except Niihau. It is widespread on other islands in Oceania and also occurs on Madagascar.

Habitat: On the Hawaiian Islands this is one of the "house geckos." Although it has been eradicated in some places by true house geckos (genus *Hemidactylus*), the stump-toed gecko is still a familiar sight on warehouses, on docks, and in piles of lumber, palm fronds, and other debris. It may also be found on trees and beneath rocks.

Size: This heavy-bodied gecko is adult at 3½–4½ inches in total length. Hatchlings are just under 2 inches long.

Stump-toed gecko. Photo by Jon Boone

Identifying features: This parthenogenetic gecko is capable of a great degree of metachrosis. While foraging at night, it may be so light in color that it appears white. When inactive during the daytime it is usually of some shade of gray with small paired lighter spots dorsally. A light stripe runs from the tip of the snout to the tympanum. The belly is off-white to very light yellow. This gecko has 4 large chin shields, the medial pair the largest;, divided under-toe lamellae, and broad subcaudal scales. The skin of this gecko tears very easily. It should not be handled.

Similar species: Its stocky countenance and large chin shields should differentiate this gecko from other species. The Indo-Pacific gecko may be the most similar in appearance, but it is slim, lacks enlarged chin shields, and has a rather bright yellow or orange belly.

ADDITIONAL SUBSPECIES

None.

TROPICAL ASIAN GECKOS, GENUS *GEKKO*

Like so many other Old World gecko genera, this genus is represented in the United States by only a single species, the tokay gecko. It is known to be established in south Florida and on Oahu, Hawaii. On spring and summer nights, the calls of this nocturnal lizard can be heard emanating from the hollows of roadside trees and occasionally from dwellings. This gecko can and will bite painfully if it is carelessly restrained. The tokay gecko has been purposely released in many areas of the country in the futile hope that it would rid homes of roaches. Many geckos escaped, but only those in the subtropical area of Florida and in Hawaii are long-term survivors.

43. Tokay Gecko
Gekko gecko

Abundance/Range: This arboreal gecko seems firmly established and quite common in certain areas of Oahu. The tokay gecko is of Asian origin.

Habitat: The tokay gecko is occasionally seen on buildings and power poles but

Tokay gecko

is most common in large shade trees, including palms. It is particularly common on trees with hollows or deep crevices where it can hide safely during the day.

Size: This is the largest gecko now found in the United States. In fact, at 12 inches in length, it is one of the largest species in the world. The young are a bit more than 3 inches long at hatching.

Identifying features: The gray body has orange and white markings and many tuberculate scales. The protuberant eyes may vary from yellow green to orange. The pupils are complex and vertically elliptical. The toepads are large and easily visible.

Voice: Males produce a loud, sharp "geck-geck-geck, geck-o, geck-o, geck-o-o-ooo" call. They vocalize most persistently on warm spring and summer nights.

Similar species: None.

Comments: Communal nests, some containing hundreds of eggs, are common. If threatened with capture, tokays open their mouths widely, "growl" with a drawn out "geccccck" and may actually jump toward an offending object, such as a hand, in an effort to bite. They will retain their grip with a bulldog-like tenacity.

ADDITIONAL SUBSPECIES

None in Hawaii.

HOUSE GECKOS, GENUS *HEMIDACTYLUS*

This genus is a huge assemblage of nocturnal, arboreal, Old World geckos. Three species occur in Hawaii; of these, one, the Mediterranean gecko, has a vast, still expanding, but spotty range across the southern United States. The Mediterranean gecko is so adept at seeking cover during the cold days of winter that it has been able to expand its range far beyond areas previously colonized by other gecko species. The geckos in this genus have expanded toepads with divided lamellae and, as indicated by their common name, are firmly associated with the walls of houses and other buildings. They may often be seen on warm nights hunting for insects that are drawn to windows and walls by house lights.

The common Indo-Pacific house gecko is an all female, parthenogenetic species.

44. Common House Gecko

Hemidactylus frenatus

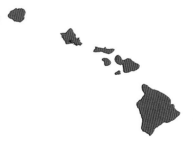

Abundance/Range: This is a well established and common gecko species on all of the main Hawaiian Islands. It is native to tropical Asia, but is now a tropicopolitan (cosmopolitan in the tropics) species.

Habitat: The walls of buildings.

Size: Although most seen are in the 3–4-inch size range, this gecko is known to attain a length of 4½ inches.

Identifying features: Dorsally this species is ashy gray with an irregular, often linear and obscure pattern of lighter or darker pigment. It becomes very light at night. Ventrally it is nearly white. A gray lateral line may be present. The scales of the body are mostly smooth, but there are six rows of rather pronounced spiny scales on its tail.

Voice: A barely audible squeak is voiced by restrained or combating males.

Similar species: This gecko may be easily confused with the Indo-Pacific gecko. However, the latter has a yellow to orange belly. The Mediterranean gecko has tuberculate body scales.

Common house gecko

ADDITIONAL SUBSPECIES

None.

45. Indo-Pacific Gecko

Hemidactylus garnotii

Abundance/Range: This is an abundant gecko on all of the main Hawaiian Islands. It is native to southeast Asia.

Habitat: Buildings, trees, fences, and similar structures are all suitable habitat for the Indo-Pacific gecko.

Size: This interesting gecko is adult at 3¾–5 inches in total length. Hatchlings are about 2 inches long.

Identifying features: Dorsally, this delicate-appearing gecko varies from a rather dark grayish brown (days) to a translucent flesh white (nights). There may or may not be indications of darker or lighter spotting. If present, the spotting is often strongest on the dorsal surface of the tail. The belly is yellowish and the underside of the tail is often a rich orange. The

Indo-Pacific gecko

body is covered with tiny nontuberculate scales. There is a row of enlarged scales along each side of the tail.

Voice: Although it is the males of most gecko species that are vocal, individuals of this all-female species also produce weak squeaks.

Similar species: The stump-toed gecko also has a yellowish belly but it is a robust, heavy-bodied species. The Indonesian tree gecko has orange under the tail but is very slender and has no spiny scales on the tail.

Comments: *H. garnotii* is a parthenogenetic (unisexual—all female) species. Even though unisexual, motions of courtship are indulged in and may, in fact, be necessary to stimulate egg development. Several sets of two eggs are produced annually by each breeding individual. Where temperatures remain suitably warm, this species can breed year round. The eggs are placed in crevices, on windowsills, or beneath ground debris.

ADDITIONAL SUBSPECIES

None.

46. Mediterranean Gecko
Hemidactylus turcicus

Abundance/Range: This abundant gecko is now widespread but locally distributed from coast to coast in the southern continental United States and in Hawaii.

Habitat: This gecko is strongly tied to human habitations. However, it may also inhabit trash piles and dumps.

Size: Although usually smaller, this species occasionally nears 5 inches in total length. Hatchlings are nearly 2 inches in total length.

Identifying features: The dorsal tubercles are prominent and most abundant on the upper sides. Those on the tail are conical. Mediterranean geckos are darker by day (brownish to gray) than by night (light gray to pasty white). Somewhat darker, irregular dorsal markings are usually visible but may disappear at night. The venter is white.

Voice: The males of this species make weak squeaking sounds. They may vocalize during territorial scuffles or when captured by human or other predators.

Mediterranean gecko

Similar species: None. The warty skin and expanded toetips of the Mediterranean gecko are diagnostic.

Comments: Look for this common gecko on still, humid nights near the outer perimeter of the halos produced by porch lights. They are shy and more difficult to approach on breezy or cool nights than on warm, still, humid nights.

ADDITIONAL SUBSPECIES

None have been identified in the U.S. populations.

TREE GECKOS; GENUS *HEMIPHYLLODACTYLUS*

This is a genus of four species of small geckos indigenous to tropical Asia and Oceania. A single species has colonized Hawaii. Unlike many other small Old World geckos, the tree geckos are entirely at home in forested areas and are not dependent on buildings as suitable habitat. The Indonesian tree gecko is an all-female, parthenogenetic species. Several clutches of two eggs each are laid each year in a secluded deposition site. Tree holes and space behind loosened bark on still-standing trees are typical egg-deposition sites and also commonly used as hiding places by the adults.

47. Indonesian Tree Gecko

Hemiphyllodactylus typus typus

Abundance/Range: This gecko is so secretive and well camouflaged that it is difficult to assess its status. It is probably not rare, but is easily overlooked. However, it has been suggested that it has dwindled in numbers in Hawaii since the various house geckos have become established. It occurs on all of the main Hawaiian Islands.

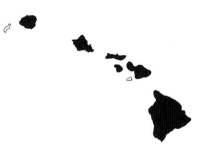

Habitat: This is more of a forest species than a house gecko. It is often seen on the trunks of large trees and more rarely on walls.

Indonesian tree gecko. Photo by Fred Kraus

Size: The smallest of the Hawaiian geckos, the tree gecko is adult at a slender 2½–3½ inches in length. Hatchlings are about 1¾ inches long.

Identifying features: This is an olive brown to olive gray lizard with no well-defined markings. Several pairs of small paired light dots are usually visible on the nape. The slender tail is vaguely banded. A thin dark stripe from the tip of the snout to the shoulder is usually visible. A pair of light-edged dark ocelli are usually visible at the base of the tail. There are no enlarged chin shields; the under-toe lamellae are divided; the innermost toe on the forefeet is rudimentary; and there are no whorls, spinose scales, or broadened scales beneath the tail. The belly is light and the undersurface of the tail is orangish. At night, when its color is the lightest, the lizard appears translucent.

Voice: The vocalizations of this gecko are very soft chirping clicks.

Similar species: The Indo-Pacific gecko also has orange under the tail, but the tail is flanged along the edges with spiny scales.

ADDITIONAL SUBSPECIES

None in Hawaii.

SCALY-TOED GECKOS, GENUS *LEPIDODACTYLUS*

This is a genus consisting of about 30 species of small to medium-sized geckos indigenous to Asia, Micronesia, Polynesia, and Australia. The under-toe (subdigital) lamellae may be either divided or undivided. The claws are large and nonretractile. Only a single species, the mourning gecko, now very widely distributed, occurs in the United States. It has been reported from Florida and California but is most firmly established only in Hawaii. Although some populations comprise both sexes, those on the Hawaiian Islands are all females that reproduce through parthenogenesis.

48. Mourning Gecko

Lepidodactylus lugubris

Abundance/Range: This common gecko is found on all of the main and many of the lesser Hawaiian Islands. It also occurs in regions as diverse as Australia and Costa Rica, but is probably indigenous to the islands of Oceania.

Habitat: In populated areas this is a "house gecko," while in more rural areas it is a gecko of the trees.

Size: Mourning geckos are adult at only 2¾–3¼ inches in total length. The tail is slightly longer than the snout-vent length.

Identifying features: This is a small, smooth-skinned cream or tan to olive gray, or tan *and* olive gray to reddish gecko with prominent dark-edged light dorsal W's. A dark bar crosses the snout from eye to eye. There is also a dark ocular stripe from the tip of the snout to the rear of the jaw. The belly is cream to very light yellow. There are 5 rows of moderately enlarged chin scales decreasing in size from front to back. The innermost subdigital lammelae are undivided, but the distal lamellae are divided. The tail has obscure whorls.

Similar species: Indonesian tree geckos lack the dorsal markings. Indo-Pacific geckos have yellow bellies and are orange beneath the tail.

Mourning gecko

ADDITIONAL SUBSPECIES

None.

DAY GECKOS, GENUS *PHELSUMA*

At least three species of this large Madagascan and East African gecko genus are established on Hawaii. Two are small species and one is large. Unlike most other typical geckos, the day geckos are diurnal and are often seen basking in the sunlight. Although alert and wary when encountered in uninhabited areas, in populated areas day geckos become accustomed to people and will allow rather close approach.

When warm and content, day geckos literally glisten. Most are a vivid Kelly green with highlights of blue, yellow, and rust. Although these geckos may be found on buildings, they are more adapted to life among the surrounding greenery.

Besides insects the day geckos feed on sap and pollen.

Adult, gravid females of the geckos in this genus have an endolymphatic (chalk) sac on each side of the neck. It is thought that the calcareous material contained therein is important to the formation of the egg shells.

49. Orange-spotted Day Gecko

Phelsuma guimbeaui guimbeaui

Abundance/Range: This is a well-established but locally found gecko on Oahu, Hawaii. It is native to Mauritius.

Habitat: On Oahu this gecko may be seen on the trunks of banana plants, palms, and shade trees. It is only occasionally seen on walls and fences.

Size: Males are larger than females. Males may near 7 inches in length but are usually smaller. Females are about 5 inches long. Hatchlings are 2½ inches long.

Identifying features: This heavy-bodied gecko is somewhat flattened in appearance. Content adults have a ground color of rich green (somewhere between Kelly and forest green). There is a turquoise overlay on the shoulders and numerous orange spots on the head, back, and tail. The tip of the tail is also suffused with blue. A thin, orange, often broken dorsolateral stripe is present on each side. If stressed this gecko dulls to gray or may remain dull green with black patches on the dorsum. Hatchlings are pinkish

Orange-spotted day gecko

gray with paired light spots from nape to tailtip. An orange stripe extends on each side of the snout from nostril to eye, and an orange bar crosses the bridge of the snout. Bruises and tears in the skin will show dull green until fully healed. The belly is greenish white. The scales of the back and sides are granular. The large eyes are lidless and have round pupils. Toepads are strongly developed.

Voice: This gecko can squeak but is usually silent.

Similar species: Anoles lack orange markings and tend to be compressed somewhat from side to side rather than flattened from top to bottom. The golddust day gecko has an overlay of gold flecking on the shoulders.

ADDITIONAL SUBSPECIES

None in Hawaii.

50. Golddust Day Gecko

Phelsuma laticauda laticauda

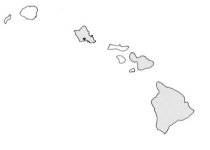

Abundance/Range: A native of Madagascar, this small, beautiful, diurnal gecko is documented on Hawaii, Maui, and Oahu, and may now be present on other islands. It is reasonably common.

Habitat: This gecko may be seen on banana trees, bamboos, palms, and other trees near buildings, as well as on the buildings themselves.

Size: This small day gecko is adult at about 4½ inches in length. The hatchlings are 1½ inches long.

Identifying features: The ground color of this gecko is a bright green. An overlay of gold-dusting is present on the nape, shoulders, and anterior trunk. Transverse orange bars are present on the top of the head. An orange bridle crosses the bridge of the nose, and the ends extend nearly to each eye. Some turquoise shading is often present near each eye. Orange spots and longitudinal bars are present from midback to above the hind legs. Bruises and tears in the skin will show dull green until fully healed. The belly is whitish. Stress will cause the lizard to assume a much darker,

Golddust day gecko

less pleasant green. The large, lidless eyes have round pupils. The toes are broadly expanded. This gecko is an agile and persistent climber.

Hatchlings are usually a dull olive green.

Voice: Sparring males often voice weak squeaks.

Similar species: Green anoles are more slender and lack both the gold-dusting and the orange dorsal spots. The orange-spotted day gecko lacks the gold dusting on the shoulders.

ADDITIONAL SUBSPECIES

None in Hawaii.

51. Giant Day Gecko

Phelsuma madagascariensis grandis

Abundance/Range: A native of Mada-
gascar, this large diurnal gecko was documented on the island of Hawaii in 2004. Its relative abundance is yet (2008) unknown.

Habitat: This gecko may be seen on ba-nana trees, bamboos, palms, and other ornamental trees as well as fences and buildings.

Giant day gecko, adult

Giant day gecko, hatchling

Size: One of the largest of the day geckos, this taxon may attain a length of 11 inches. Most adults are between 8 and 10½ inches in length. Males are larger than females. The hatchlings are 2 inches long.

Identifying features: Although hatchlings and stressed adults may be a dull green, the more usual ground color of this gecko is a bright Kelly green. Hatchlings are liberally marked dorsally on head, trunk, and tail with irregular barring and/or spotting of bright orange. The dorsal head marking is usually a well-defined V, the point being just posterior to the nostrils. An orange bar extending from the nostril to the eye is present on each side of the face. The orange color is present also on the lateral interstitial skin (the skin between the scales). Some turquoise shading may be present near each eye. The bright green adults tend to have fewer orange dorsal markings and seldom show any indication of orange on the sides. The orange dorsal spots are usually most prominent on the posterior back and are absent from the tail. Bruises and tears in the skin will show dull green until fully healed. The belly is whitish. The eyes are large, lidless, and have round pupils. The toes are broadly expanded. This gecko is an agile and persistent climber.

Voice: Sparring or restrained males often voice quite audible squeaks.

Similar species: Green anoles are more slender and lack the orange dorsal spots. The orange-spotted day gecko lacks the gold dusting on the shoulders.

ADDITIONAL SUBSPECIES

None in Hawaii.

LEAF-TOED GECKOS, GENUS *PHYLLODACTYLUS*

This genus contains more than 45 small geckos, many of which are rock dwellers and all of which are colored much like the strata on which they dwell. They move rapidly over the faces of the rocks with a curious straddle-legged gait. They are flattened and access crevices and fissures easily. A single species ranges northward from Baja into south central California. Although a concerted search on desert outcroppings and escarpments is usually necessary to see this gecko, the species is occasionally found on paved roads that transect their range.

52. Peninsula Leaf-toed Gecko

Phyllodactylus nocticolus

Abundance/Range: Although this gecko is fairly common, it is of spotty distribution. It is found from central Riverside County, California, southward to central Baja California Sur.

Peninsula leaf-toed gecko

Habitat: Cliff faces, escarpments, outcroppings, boulder fields and rocky canyons are home to this gecko.

Size: Although most adults of this species are 3½–4½ inches long, they occasionally attain a length of 5 inches. The tail is about equal to the head and body in length. Hatchlings are about 1¾ inches in length.

Identifying features: The flattened body and head are an adaptation for life in the crevices and fissures of this gecko's rockland home. The dorsal color may be reddish, brown, or some shade of gray and closely matches the color of the rocks on which the leaf-toe is found. Obscure darker dorsal markings are present. The sides are the same color as the back. The belly is lighter than the back and sides. A claw is situated between the two fanlike toetip scales. The legs are long and sturdy.

Similar species: None in California.

ADDITIONAL SUBSPECIES

As currently understood, none.

WALL GECKOS, GENUS *TARENTOLA*

A single species of this sizable genus of nocturnal geckos now occurs in San Diego County, California. It is probable that it was introduced by the pet trade. These are heavy-bodied, strong-jawed, predatory geckos that may occasionally include a smaller gecko among their more normal insect repast. They have broadly dilated toetips, and in California they are associated with walls and piles of building rubble.

53. Moorish Wall Gecko

Tarentola mauritanica

Abundance/Range: Unknown. This newly established gecko is found in isolated warehouse areas in San Diego County, California.

Habitat: In the United States, this rock-dweller has become a "house" gecko. It may be seen on the walls of dwellings and warehouses as well as in construction rubble.

Size: This heavy-bodied, big-headed gecko attains a total length of about 6 inches. Hatchlings are about 2 inches long.

Identifying features: Adults have a variable, but never brilliant color. The dorsal color varies from sandy tan to olive gray. Crossbars may be present. The dorsal scales, which are large and roughened, dictate the alternate name of "crocodile gecko." Young specimens have dark transverse bands. Tail scales are spinose, especially along the tail-edges. These geckos are paler at night than during the day. Toepads are prominent.

Voice: Males emit clicking squeaks during courtship and territorial disputes, or when the lizard is restrained.

Similar species: None in California.

ADDITIONAL SUBSPECIES

None.

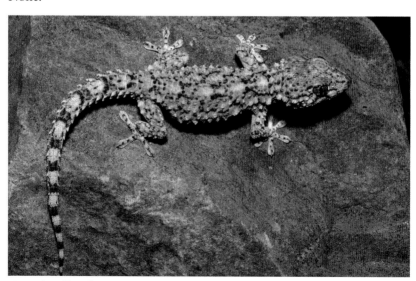

Moorish wall gecko

14

Gila Monsters

Family Helodermatidae

The Gila monster is the signature lizard species of our southwestern deserts. Fables about this large, gaudy, defensive, venomous, and protected lizard abound. Facts about it are harder to come by.

Considering the disdain with which venomous snakes are usually treated, the rigid protection offered the Gila monster comes as a bit of a surprise. But protected it is, and the Gila monster cannot be legally collected or molested (poked, prodded, handled, or moved) without a permit.

There are only two lizard species in the family Helodermatidae, the Gila monster (two subspecies) and the beaded lizard, which has several subspecies. Of the two, only the Gila monster occurs in the United States.

A Venomous Beauty

Patti and I had decided to spend a few days photographing reptiles and amphibians in south central Arizona. Our friend Regis Opferman was with us. Although Patti and I hoped to see and photograph at least one of everything, Regis had a single driving interest; he wanted to see a Gila monster, *Heloderma suspectum*, in natural habitat.

To accomplish this there is hardly any place better than Organ Pipe National Monument. But Gilas are protected, and when caught by surprise some rangers can be overly zealous, so we thought it best to make our presence and intent known to the folks who oversee and protect this magnificent park.

This we did, and as dusk fell we were back in the park, driving the remote dirt roads, taking particular care to scrutinize the washes and boulder fields carefully.

Darkness was fully upon us as we began our ascent of Ajo Mountain. Stars twinkled above, pinpoints of light in a midnight black sky. Silhouettes of giant saguaros, interspersed with an occasional example of the organ pipe cactus that gave the park its name, were barely visible in the darkness. A pygmy owl tooted. As we climbed, the road fell sharply away on the left. "It's time for a Gila," Regis said. We rounded a curve and as if on cue, just coming onto the road, fat as a pink and black sausage, was a big Gila. Regis was overjoyed. What am I saying? All of us were overjoyed.

We photographed the lizard, then stood and watched as it plodded slowly, belly dragging, into a boulder field on the opposite side of the road to be lost in the night.

GILA MONSTER, GENUS *HELODERMA*

The Gila monster is a slow-moving, lumbering lizard. It feeds on nestling rodents and ground-nesting birds, other reptiles, amphibians, eggs, and insects.

It is active by both day and night, but seems to wander most often in the early evening.

Gilas are encountered not only in natural scrubby desert and boulder strewn habitats, but also with some frequency in suburban areas of cities as large as Tucson and Phoenix, Arizona.

A Gila's tail is a fat storage organ. During times of plenty when the lizard is eating regularly and moisture is available the tail swells to its largest diameter. When times are poor, such as during drought or when prey is difficult to procure, the Gila gets nourishment from the fat storage of the tail.

A Gila's venom is produced in glands situated on the outer side of the lower jaw. Venom flows with the saliva and enters bite wounds as the lizard bites. The longer the bite, the more venom enters.

Speculation has it that, since the venom lacks predigestive enzymes and anticoagulants, it is more for defense than for overcoming prey. Although rare, human fatalities have occurred from Gila bites.

This lizard is oviparous. The 1–12 eggs (normally 2–6) are large and have a lengthy incubation period—nearly 5 months.

54. Reticulated Gila Monster

Heloderma suspectum suspectum

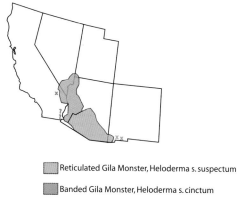

Abundance/Range: Although still fairly common in some areas, development has reduced or extirpated Gila populations in many historic areas. This is a rigidly protected subspecies that occurs in southern Arizona, immediately adjacent southwestern New Mexico, most of Sonora, Mexico, and extreme northwestern Chihuahua.

Reticulated Gila Monster, Heloderma s. suspectum

Banded Gila Monster, Heloderma s. cinctum

Habitat: This desert lizard occurs in a broad cross section of habitats. It is found in mesquite deserts and creosote flats, in dry washes, near intermittent streams, in rocky pastureland, in national parks, and in many similar habitats.

Size: A large adult may attain an overall length of 24 inches. The tail is only 65% of the snout-vent length. Hatchlings average 5 inches in length.

Identifying features: This is a very heavy-bodied, low-slung lizard with

Reticulated Gila monster

very short legs and broad head—the dachshund of American lizards, if you will. Although the pattern of the hatchlings looks very much like that of the more westerly banded Gila monster (except for the tail rings, which remain well defined), with growth comes pattern complexity. The black bands of the body fragment and become infiltrated with patches of the pink, pinkish orange, or pinkish yellow ground color, producing a complex pattern.

Similar species: None. No other lizard in the American West has the color scheme or beaded scales of the Gila monsters.

Comments: Don't allow the slow movement and rather ungainly appearance of this lizard to fool you. If startled or frightened these lizards can reverse positions or snap to the side with amazing rapidity. The bite is tenacious and the venom dangerous. Use extreme care when nearing a Gila monster!

ADDITIONAL SUBSPECIES

55. The Banded Gila Monster, *Heloderma suspectum cinctum*, is found to the west and the north of the reticulated race. Banded Gilas may be found from southern Nevada and extreme southwestern Utah to eastern California and western Arizona. This race does not undergo the body-band fragmentation as it ages, retaining instead the simple double-banded pattern of the juveniles.

Banded Gila monster

15

Iguanas and Relatives

Collared and Leopard Lizards, Iguanas, Anoles, Swifts, Tree Lizards, Earless Lizards, and Horned Lizards

These diverse lizards (plus several other groupings) are all considered iguanian lizards. All were once contained in the family Iguanidae but are now split into seven families; however, it has again been suggested that all should be reunited in the family Iguanidae. The iguanians are represented in western North America and Hawaii by four of the seven families, as follows:

- Collared and Leopard Lizards (Crotaphytidae; 7 species)
- Iguanas and Chuckwallas (Iguanidae; 4 species)
- Horned and Spiny Lizards and their relatives (Phrynosomatidae; 36 species
- Anoles (Polychrotidae; 3 species)

Iguanian Lizards: The Biggest and Most Diverse Grouping

Some are slender arborealists that are almost acrobatic in their motions. Some attain a length of more than 7 feet when fully adult. Others are short, stubby, flattened, spine studded, and terrestrial. You may see some darting nimbly over rock faces. Some are clad in colors of the leaves and others in the hues of the sands and rocks on which they dwell. Some species are fast and instantaneous in their actions and reactions while others are slow and methodical, seeming almost phlegmatic at times.

But whether they are anoles, horned lizards, typical iguanas, or fringe-toed lizards, all are considered iguanian lizards.

By virtue of the number of families and their diversity the iguanians can be a perplexing family to define. My search for the many species in the various iguanian families has drawn me to and fro across the continent and beyond.

I have seen green iguanas piled so deeply that their combined weight bends slender Brazilian peppertree branches from horizontal to vertical pendula. I have watched horned lizards emerge from their shallow pallet beneath the night-cooled sand to begin the activity of the day under the warming rays of a morning sun. And I have witnessed granite spiny lizards and chuckwallas slowly stir, then edge their way from their crevice homes to first thermoregulate and then forage. I learned by watching banded rock lizards on their granite boulders that side-blotched lizards are relished as prey. And I have stared at the dead limb of a sun-drenched creosote bush for minutes on end knowing that something was just a bit out of place but not actually seeing the anomaly until a little long-tailed brush lizard would shift its position and catch my eye.

And then there are the anoles and the fringe-toed lizards—but you can read about them just a bit farther on.

COLLARED AND LEOPARD LIZARDS, FAMILY CROTAPHYTIDAE

These are beautiful, active, predatory lizards that become bipedal when running swiftly. The collared lizards have a broad, enlarged head, a small neck, and a stocky build. Males of some species and of some populations of collared lizards have a brightly colored throat. Females are duller, but develop orange patches on their sides when they are gravid. These fade shortly after egg deposition. Both sexes of most species have two black collars on the neck. These are often interrupted on the nape.

The leopard lizards are somewhat more slender and have proportionately narrow heads. They are clad in scales of earthen tones and lack collars. Like the collared lizards, gravid female leopard lizards develop patches of orange on the sides.

The lizards of both genera are strongly cannibalistic, eating smaller lizards and an occasional small snake as well as large insects.

All collared and leopard lizards are oviparous.

Collared and Leopard Lizards, Genera *Crotaphytus* and *Gambelia*

Four species of collared lizards and three species of leopard lizards occur in the American west. The ranges of some extend well into Mexico, where additional species occur as well. None occur in either Canada or Hawaii.

The collared lizards usually favor boulder-strewn areas and escarpments. The leopard lizards are creatures of sparsely vegetated desert regions.

Each clutch comprises 2–9 eggs.

56. Great Basin Collared Lizard

Crotaphytus bicinctores

Abundance/Range: This lizard is of variable abundance, but seems relatively common for an actively cannibalistic species. It is found from eastern California and southwestern Arizona to southern Idaho.

Great Basin collared lizard, male

Habitat: This, like most collared lizards, is a species associated with desert boulder fields. It ranges from sea level to nearly 7,500 feet in elevation.

Size: Adult males may occasionally attain 13 inches in total length. The tail is about 180% of the SVL. Females are the smaller sex. Hatchlings are about 3 inches long.

Identifying features: Although one of the more quietly colored of the collared lizards, this species is, nevertheless, quite pretty.

Both sexes have a ground color of olive brown to olive green. There are numerous narrow terra-cotta bands. Both the ground color and the light bands are liberally sprinkled with tiny white flecks. The color is brightest when the lizard is well warmed. The limbs and tail are prominently reticulated with light lines against an olive ground. The tail is flattened laterally and has a light stripe along the top. Males have a dark spotted gray to bluish gray throat with a central black spot. There are 2 well-formed collars. The belly is grayish with black groin patches. Females are smaller and paler in color. Hatchlings are vividly patterned with orangish crossbands and black dorsal spots against a ground color of olive brownish gray. The interior of the mouth is light.

Similar species: These lizards are not easily mistaken for lizards of other groups, but may be mistaken for other species of collared lizards. Use range as an identification tool. Also please see accounts 57, 58, and 59. The various collared species of spiny lizards have only a single collar.

Comments: This lizard is fast, and if cornered, feisty. Carelessly restrained adults can pinch a finger painfully. These collared lizards can be seen sprawled atop sun-bathed rocks during the morning hours. If startled, they usually seek shelter beneath a rock (often their basking rock), in a mammal burrow, or amid the rubble of a packrat nest.

57. Eastern Collared Lizard

Crotaphytus collaris

Abundance/Range: This beautifully colored collared lizard is a familiar sight from Missouri and Arkansas to Texas, Utah, and Arizona.

Habitat: This is a rock-dwelling lizard of semiarid to arid areas. Look for it basking conspicuously on rocky hillsides, escarpments, and lower regions of talus, on rocks tumbled from road cuts, along dry washes, and in other similar habitats. It prefers elevations from a few hundred feet above sea level to 9,800 feet.

Size: Occasional adult males may exceed 12 inches in length (record, 14 inches), but are usually smaller. Adult females are normally smaller than the males. The tail is about 180% of the SVL. Healthy collared lizards are chunky and big headed. Hatchlings are about 3 inches long.

Identifying features: The males of this collared lizard are among the most spectacular of American lizards. Both males and females are especially brightly colored during the spring and summer breeding season. The dorsal color is darkest when the lizard is cold or inactive. The dorsal and lateral scales are tiny and granular. Ventral scales are larger and often keeled. There is a single skin fold across the throat. Males are a bright bluish green to green dorsally and laterally. Narrow yellow bands are sometimes present. The head and forefeet may be gray, off-white, or some shade of yellow. The throat is blue green. Colors are brightest when the lizards are reproductively active. Black apical spots are often present. The dorsal surface of the tail may be of the same color as the dorsum, or may be darker. Tiny

Eastern collared lizard, male, yellow headed form

Eastern collared lizard, male, green form

Eastern collared lizard, female

light spots and reticulations may be present. A prominent double black collar is present. This may be interrupted on the nape. The belly is white. The interior of the mouth is black.

Females are lighter, often of a tan color or pale greenish tan, but reproductively active individuals are spotted and barred with fire to red orange laterally.

Hatchlings are prettily patterned with precisely delineated wide brown and narrow yellow bars. With growth, the edges quickly obscure.

Similar species: See accounts 56, 58, and 59 for descriptions of other collared lizards. Spiny lizards have only a single collar and keeled, pointed body scales.

Comments: These are persistently heliothermic lizards that bask frequently and for long periods. They sit conspicuously atop rocks and boulders, with the largest and most dominant male choosing the highest vantage point. As they become warmed, they straighten their legs and lift their body high above the sun-warmed rock surface, often tipping their toes upward (and standing only on their heels) to reduce heat absorption as much as possible. When overly warm they will cool in the shadows or in their burrow for a short time, then resume basking.

Collared lizards often dig their own burrows beneath the boulders on which they display, but may seek shelter beneath surface debris or in packrat nests and burrows as well.

ADDITIONAL SUBSPECIES

None.

58. Sonoran Collared Lizard

Crotaphytus nebrius

Abundance/Range: This is a fairly common species that ranges southward from southwestern and south central Arizona to southern Sonora, Mexico.

Habitat: Rocky clearings, boulder fields, and the base of low, rock-strewn outcroppings are home to this lizard.

Size: Adult are 9½–11 inches in total length;

Sonoran collared lizard, male

an occasional male may reach 13 inches. The tail is about 180% of the SVL. Hatchlings are about 3¼ inches long.

Identifying features: This is the least colorful of the collared lizards of the United States. The dorsum is cream, tan, or light brown with a profusion of light spots on the back and sides. The spots are largest on the back. The throat is gray and light banded. The double black collar is prominent. Breeding males often develop a suffusion of orange on the belly and in the center of the throat. Females are less colorful except when gravid, when brilliant orange lateral bands are formed. This lizard is found to an elevation of at least 4,800 feet on the summit of Ajo Mountain.

Similar species: Please see accounts 56, 57, and 59 for discussions of other collared lizards.

ADDITIONAL SUBSPECIES

None.

59. Baja (Black) Collared Lizard

Crotaphytus vestigium

Abundance/Range: Although not actually uncommon, this collared lizard has a small and
spotty distribution in the United States. It ranges
southward from Riverside County, California, to
central Baja California Sur.

Habitat: This, like most collared lizards, is a species associated with desert boulder fields. This
pretty collared lizard is found from sea level to
4,000 feet in elevation.

Size: Adult males may attain a length of 12½
inches. The tail is about 180% of the SVL. Females are smaller. Hatchlings
are about 3 inches in length.

Identifying features: Although one of the more quietly colored of the
collared lizards, this species is, nevertheless, quite pretty. The Baja collared
lizard is a bit more colorful in southern Baja than in the United States.

Both sexes have a ground color of warm fawn brown. The color is most
intense when the lizard is well warmed. Large cream, yellow, or black
spots and bars are present on the back and sides against a lighter reticulum. The brown tail is reticulated on the sides with light tan and bears
a light stripe along the upper surface. The crown is fawn, and the sides

Baja collared lizard, male

Baja collared lizard, female

of the face are fawn reticulated with yellow. The limbs are spotted. Both collars are interrupted dorsally. The belly is tan to olive tan. Males have large black inguinal patches. The throat is light gray with ocelli resembling leopard spots and a black-centered blue central patch. Females are smaller and tannish gray. The orange markings developed by gravid females are very vivid. Hatchlings are tan with light markings.

Similar species: Please compare the collared lizards in accounts 56, 57, and 58.

ADDITIONAL SUBSPECIES

None.

60. Cope's Leopard Lizard

Gambelia copeii

Abundance/Range: Although common in Baja, this is a rare lizard in the United States. It barely crosses the border into extreme southern San Diego County, California, near the towns of Campo and Jacumba.

Habitat: This is a species of open chaparral and other sparsely vegetated desert habitats.

Cope's leopard lizard, breeding female

Size: This large lizard may reach a total length of 15 inches. Females are the larger sex. Hatchlings are about 3½ inches long.

Identifying features: This is a large tan to gray lizard with a long nose and a complex pattern of dark spots and light dots. The dark spots may be prominent or so obscure as to be nearly invisible, but when present, are usually *not* bordered by light pigment and are most numerous and largest posteriorly. The top of the head is unspotted. There are (about) 7 narrow light bars across the back, all divided medially by a light vertebral stripe. An overlay of white dots from nape to tail is present. The limbs bear dark spots and light dots. The surface of the tail is very prominently banded. The belly is white; the underside of the tail is almost white on nonbreeding animals but fire orange on gravid females. Gravid females also develop orange bars laterally.

Similar species: The long-nosed leopard lizard is very similar but usually more strongly patterned, especially on the anterior back. The head is also spotted. Compare the leopard lizards in accounts 61 and 62.

Comments: Because this lizard is so easily confused with the long-nosed leopard lizard, its population statistics in the United States are virtually unknown.

ADDITIONAL SUBSPECIES

None.

61. Blunt-nosed Leopard Lizard

Gambelia sila

Abundance/Range: Because of habitat modifications (this equates to loss of habitat to agriculture and development), this lizard is now of endangered status. It is found in and around California's San Joaquin Valley.

Habitat: Grassy fields, open desert, even alkali flats in California's San Joaquin Valley are the range of this leopard lizard.

Size: At an adult size of 9½ inches, this is the smallest of the leopard lizards. Males are larger than females. Hatchlings are about 2¾ inches long.

Identifying features: Although dorsal spotting usually predominates, some examples of this species have very prominent dorsal bars with spots in the interspaces. The spots are usually rounded and have light edges.

Blunt-nosed leopard lizard, female

Blunt-nosed leopard lizard, male

The ground color is tan, brown, or grayish. This blends well with the background when the lizard is inactive. The belly is white. The throat is white with longitudinal gray streaks. Gravid females have orange bars on the sides, and the underside of the tail is orange. Except for being somewhat smaller, or when they are gravid, females are very similar to the male in appearance. Gravid females have bright orange spots and bars on the sides, and the underside of the tail is brilliant orange. Hatchlings are prominently barred and are profusely spotted with brown or deep red. **Similar species:** Other leopard lizards. Please see accounts 60 and 62 for discussions of the other species.

ADDITIONAL SUBSPECIES

None.

62. Long-nosed Leopard Lizard

Gambelia wislizenii

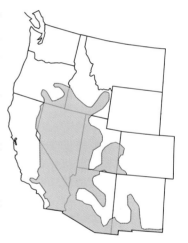

Abundance/Range: This lizard is rather generally distributed, but not present in great population densities. It is found from western Texas southward into Mexico and northwestward to southeastern Oregon and southern Idaho.
Habitat: Sparsely vegetated, sandy and gravelly plains are the preferred habitat of leopard lizards. They may sit quietly in the shade of a mesquite or creosote bush in the hottest weather, bask in apparent abandon in the warming sunshine on cool mornings, or dash bipedally from grass clump to grass clump when foraging.
Size: Although most examples are between 9 and 12 inches in total length, the record length for this aridland speedster is 15⅛ inches. Females are the larger sex. Hatchlings are about 3½ inches long.
Identifying features: The dorsal and lateral colors of this attractive lizard blend splendidly with the substrates on which it is found. Despite the common name, the streaking and striping of this lizard is often more evi-

Long-nosed leopard lizard, female

dent than the spotting. The light ground color of the leopard lizard may be tinged with olive or gray. The rounded spots are largest dorsally. At cool temperatures, or when the lizard is inactive, the colors are darkest. Some of the pattern combinations are as follows:

- Dorsal pattern of 7–10 complete (not broken vertebrally) straw yellow bars with light-edged dark oval spots in the interspaces. Tail barred, but with a light stripe on dorsal surface.
- Dorsal pattern of 7–10 straw yellow bars broken vertebrally and often offset with light-edged dark oval spots in the interspaces. Tail barred, but with a light stripe on dorsal surface.
- Dorsal bars obscured. Profuse brown and orange spots offset by barely lighter scales. Tail spotted on sides and with a light stripe on dorsal surface.
- Occasional examples have a pattern fragmented into spots and bars of unusual shapes and lacking light outlines.

The head and limbs are spotted. The belly is white. The throat is white with longitudinal gray streaks. Gravid females have orange bars on the sides, and the underside of the tail is orange. Except for being somewhat larger, or when they are gravid, females are very similar to the male in appearance. Gravid females have bright orange spots and bars on the sides and the underside of the tail is brilliant orange. Hatchlings are prominently barred and profusely spotted with brown or deep red.

Similar species: See accounts 60 and 61 for the other leopard lizards.

Comments: This lizard often darts from patch to patch of vegetation, moving bipedally when at full speed, and stopping abruptly. It may allow fairly close approach before dashing away, but at other times will dash off the moment it spies a person. When at rest in the dappled shade of a sagebrush or creosote bush, the lizard is difficult to see in the camouflage provided by the earthen hues.

ADDITIONAL SUBSPECIES

None.

IGUANAS AND CHUCKWALLAS, FAMILY IGUANIDAE

The green iguana has been established in Hawaii since the 1950s. Initially restricted to the island of Oahu, it has now been found on Hawaii and on Kauai. The green iguana hales from several different Latin American countries.

The Sonoran spiny-tailed iguana is indigenous to northwestern Mexico and has been long established as an "experimental colony" on the grounds of the Arizona-Sonora Desert Museum.

Both iguanas exceed 36 inches in length, and males of the green iguana may more than double that size. They are, therefore, the largest lizards now known to occur within the coverage area of this book.

Chuckwallas and the desert iguana are native to our southwest and to northwestern Mexico, including the Baja Peninsula.

These lizards are all oviparous, and all are predominantly herbivorous. Adults of both of the large iguana species are very strong and if restrained improperly will bite, slap with their tail, and scratch painfully and effectively. Handle adults with extreme care.

Spiny-tailed Iguana, Genus *Ctenosaura*

Ranging from northern Mexico (including many islands and the Baja Peninsula) to Panama, the spiny-tailed iguanas vary in size from 8-inch-long arboreal species to boulder-field dwellers of more than 4 feet. Only a single species of spiny-tailed iguana occurs in the American west. It is restricted in distribution to the grounds (or possibly the grounds and the immediate proximity) of the Arizona-Sonora Desert Museum (ASDM) in Tucson, Arizona.

From 15 to more than 30 eggs are laid in a single clutch each spring.

63. Sonoran Spiny-tailed Iguana

Ctenosaura hemilopha macrolopha

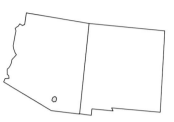

Abundance/Range: Although fairly common on the grounds of the Arizona-Sonora Desert Museum, this iguana does not seem to have spread beyond the site of its introduction. It is native to Sonora, Sinaloa, the Baja Peninsula, and some of the islands of Mexico.

Habitat: This huge lizard may be seen on rockpiles and walls, atop cages, on sidewalks, or atop saguaros in the ASDM. Young climb frequently and well.

Size: Hatchlings are about 7 inches in total length. Adult females commonly attain a total length of 3 feet; adult males may near or slightly exceed 4 feet.

Identifying features: Hatchlings are grayish but change to a bright green within just a few days. With growth they gradually assume the adult coloration of black bars on a tan or olive gray ground. Breeding adults may assume enhanced colors, and males become very territorial—bobbing and

Sonoran spiny-tailed iguana, adult coloration

Sonoran spiny-tailed iguana, juvenile coloration

strutting—during the breeding season. Stressed (cold, ill, subordinate) or inactive individuals may be almost black. Females are always less colorful than males. A vertebral crest, most prominent on adult males, is present.

Similar species: Baby spiny-tailed iguanas may be mistaken for baby green iguanas; however, the latter lack the whorls of large, spiny caudal scales. Adult spiny-tails are gray with black bands; adult green iguanas are of some shade of green.

Comments: These alert and wary lizards come to know their home territory well. They may be seen basking, head raised well away from the ground, on boulders, on piles of rubble and building materials, and even on the paved trails. They retire to burrows at night and in inclement weather, and dart to the burrows if frightened during the day.

Desert Iguana, Genus *Dipsosaurus*

The single species in this genus may be encountered in aridland habitats over much of the southwestern United States, northwestern Mexico, and the length of the Baja Peninsula. The desert iguana is predominantly herbivorous, consuming both leaves and blossoms of creosote bush and other desert herbs and shrubs. Some insects are also eaten. This alert lizard is quite heat tolerant and may be active in dappled shade even in the midday heat.

A normal clutch consists of 3–5 eggs.

64. Northern Desert Iguana

Dipsosaurus dorsalis dorsalis

Abundance/Range: This is an abundant species in the creosote flats (United States) and thornscrub (Mexico). It is found from southeastern California and southern Nevada to the southern tip of the Baja Peninsula and northwestern Sinaloa.

Habitat: Sandy and gravelly flats where creosote bush is the hub for kangaroo rat middens is a favorite habitat for this iguana. It is tolerant of a great deal of heat, and may be seen out foraging on very hot days. It may clamber up into shrubs both to feed and to escape untenably hot sand-surface temperatures. It also enters burrows (both of rodents and of its own making) to moderate its body temperature. It occurs from below sea level in interior desert valleys to about 5,000 feet in elevation.

Size: Most adults are between 12 and 14 inches long, but they may occasionally attain a 16-inch length. The thick tail is about 160% of the SVL. Hatchlings are about 3¾ inches long.

Identifying features: This is a quietly colored but attractive lizard. It is heavy bodied, has a proportionately small head, a heavy tail, and well-formed limbs. When walking or running, it carries itself well away from the ground. When frightened, the desert iguana inflates its body and often looks twice the size it really is. The dorsal scales are fine and granular.

Northern desert iguana

Those on the belly are larger and overlap each other. A weakly serrate crest runs from nape well onto the tail.

The ground color is gray to brown above with bars or a reticulum of burgundy or darker brown. Small, lighter gray or tan ocelli may form regular bands over the sides and dorsum. Brownish bars extend downward onto the gray belly. The sides of the belly become suffused with rose or buff during the breeding season.

Similar species: There are no other lizards in the region having a heavy body and similar markings of light tan or gray and burgundy over a darker tan ground color.

Comments: Desert iguanas are sun worshippers in the most literal sense. Simply put, no matter how warm the weather, if no sun is shining, desert iguanas are seldom active. Conversely, these stout lizards may be out and active far into a day when the heat would send other species into shelter. Although usually darting about on four legs, if hard-pressed they occasionally run bipedally.

ADDITIONAL SUBSPECIES

None.

Green Iguana, Genus *Iguana*

This is an impressive and unmistakable lizard. Adults attain a relatively massive body size. The green iguana is of Latin American origin. It is a popular pet species. The only other species in the genus is the endangered West Indian iguana.

A clutch contains from 15 to more than 50 eggs. Communal nesting has been witnessed.

65. Green Iguana

Iguana iguana

Abundance/Range: This lizard has been established on Oahu for about 60 years. It is now probably breeding on other main islands. It is well known but does not seem to be especially common.

Habitat: Yards, woodlands, and most

Left: Green iguana, adult male

Below: Green iguana, juvenile

habitats in between are colonized by iguanas. All sizes climb well, but also seek rocks, walls, and rubble for observation and displaying posts. Iguanas swim well and do not hesitate to take to the water if startled.

Size: Hatchlings are about 7 inches in total length. Adult females may attain 4½ feet; adult males may attain more than 6 feet in total length.

Identifying features: Healthy babies are bright green; ill ones may be brownish or yellow. Some have dark bars across the back and on the sides.

Adult coloration tends to fade, retaining a green suffusion over grayish scales. Some individually suffuse anteriorly with orange during the breeding season. A huge dewlap and vertebral crest are present. These are larger on males than on females. A large rounded scale is present on the jowls. There are no enlarged spiny scales on the tail.

Similar species: None in Hawaii.

Comments: These are alert lizards, that, if healthy, are difficult to approach. Both male and female great green iguanas are territorial and will indulge in push-ups, tail-slapping, and actual skirmishing to rout conspecific interlopers. If threatened with capture and not able to escape, adults will slap with the tail. If green iguanas are actually captured, their scratching and biting will quickly open wounds. Babies are very fast and dart quickly to safety when threatened. Green iguanas routinely bask high in trees, often in those overhanging the water. These lizards will drop considerable distances from the limbs of trees, hit the ground or water with a resounding thud, and either run or swim quickly away.

Chuckwalla, Genus *Sauromalus*

The chuckwalla is the second largest *native* lizard in the United States. It is exceeded in length only by the Gila monster.

    This large lizard is of variable color and size. In most populations the females are smaller and less colorful than the males. These heavy-bodied lizards usually emerge from their crevice or burrow hideaways only after the sun has warmed the landscape. Then the lizards are usually seen basking on sun-drenched boulders.

    A clutch usually contains between 4 and 11 eggs.

66. Common Chuckwalla

Sauromalus ater (formerly *Sauromalus obesus*)

Abundance/Range: This is a widespread but not very common iguanian lizard species. It is found from southern Nevada and southern Utah to central western Sonora and almost to the tip of the Baja Peninsula, Mexico.

Common chuckwalla, male, South Mountain, Ariz., form

Common chuckwalla, male, red-backed form

Habitat: This is a rock-dwelling lizard that, despite its size and quite considerable girth, is adept at sidling into fissures and crevices when disturbed. Because of its propensity for sidling between roughened rocks and inflating its body, the skin of the chuckwalla often appears scruffy and abraded. Look for this lizard in boulder fields, along creviced road cuts, on escarpments and outcroppings, and anywhere else where there is sufficient rock cover.

Size: In length and girth, of lizards of the United States, the chuckwalla is second only to the Gila monster in body mass. Its loose, folded skin

Common chuckwalla, juvenile and female coloration

gives it the appearance of a size 6 lizard in a size 8 skin. The adult size is 10–14 inches, but occasional examples may near 17 inches in length. The blunt-tipped tail is about 110% of the SVL. Females are the smaller sex. Hatchlings are about 4 inches in length.

Identifying features: The loose skin and obese appearance should identify this lizard. No matter the body color, the head is usually the darkest part of the lizard. Here are a few of the various color morphs of males:

- all-black head, body, and limbs, fire orange tail (near Phoenix, Arizona)
- as above but with yellow tail (some areas of eastern California)
- black head, black limbs, red trunk, yellowish tail (southern Arizona)
- black head and dark limbs, yellow trunk and tail (south central California)
- black head and limbs, gray to red trunk, light gray tail (near Lake Mead, Arizona and Utah)

Regardless of their population, females and juveniles are usually less colorful and often strongly banded with brown on olive. The tail, also banded, is the same color as the body. An exception is the Lake Mead population, where juveniles may be largely red in color.

Similar species: None in the United States.

Comments: This is a sun-loving herbivore. You may see chuckwallas basking quietly on sun-bathed rocks so hot they are uncomfortable to touch. When disturbed, "chucks" will usually scuttle to and enter a nearby crevice. If further disturbed, they will inflate their body and rely on the sandpapery texture of the scales pressing against the rock to prevent their forcible withdrawal. Wherever present within the range of the chuck-walla, the leaves and blossoms of creosote bush play an important part in the lizard's diet.

ADDITIONAL SUBSPECIES

As currently understood, none.

EARLESS, ROCK, HORNED, SPINY, FRINGE-TOED, TREE, AND SIDE-BLOTCHED LIZARDS, FAMILY PHRYNOSOMATIDAE

Although of diverse appearance, the lizards of this family are actually similar in many morphological respects. Species vary in appearance from the squat, terrestrial, horned lizards (most of which are so adorned with horns and spines that they appear like animated cacti) to the slender, highly arboreal, tree lizards. Between these extremes are the rather typical-appearing spiny, earless, rock, and side-blotched lizards, which may be arboreal, saxicolous, or terrestrial, depending on species.

The lizards of this subfamily have stylized breeding and territorial displays that include head-bobs and push-ups. None have expanded digital pads, and none are adept at changing color (although most assume a darker color when cold than when hot). Some genera lack ear openings.

The males of many species have blue, green, or rose ventrolateral and/or throat patches. If these are present on the females, they are smaller and much less brilliant. The horned lizards lack the brilliant ventral colors.

Although the females of most phrynosomatids produce one or more clutches of eggs each year, those of some produce instead a single clutch of live young.

The Fringe-toes

The iguanian species that gave me the most trouble was the newly described Yuman Desert fringe-toed lizard, *Uma rufopunctata*. This desert speedster differs genetically from the identical-appearing Colorado Desert fringe-toed lizard that occurs just across the Colorado River in California. Although fast and rather wary, the Colorado Desert fringe-toe is easily caught, because when hard pressed it usually dives beneath the loose sand of the dunes it inhabits and remains quiet.

continued

Not so with its relative from Arizona's Yuma Desert. If startled the Yuman desert fringe-toed lizard runs. If startled again it runs farther. If it feels really hard pressed, this creature runs, then runs some more, and then, after a final glance back over its shoulder, often without a break in its stride, finally throws itself headlong into the ever-present hole of a kangaroo rat or ground squirrel, disappears, and remains there for very long periods. Out of the dozens I've seen, only one made any effort to dig, and then it did so at the very mouth of a burrow. Within seconds it had popped to the surface again and darted down the hole.

I gave up, but 2008 is another year. I now know where the lizards are and when they're active. It's only the how of actually getting a definitive photograph that still has me baffled.

Zebra-tailed Lizards, Genus *Callisaurus*

In one or another of its several subspecies, this desert speedster may be encountered from northern Nevada to the southern tip of the Baja Peninsula and southern Sinaloa, Mexico. Expect to see it only on brightly sunlit days, days when the sand and rocks are so hot that the lizard may stand only on its heels or lift one foot after the other from the substrate in an effort to prevent further elevation of its body temperature.

Ear opening are present.

From 1 (north) to 3 clutches (south) of 4–9 eggs are produced annually.

67–69. Zebra-tailed Lizards

Callisaurus draconoides ssp.

Abundance/Range: These lizards are common but very wary. They often dart for cover before an observer can get a truly good look at them. They range from northwestern Nevada southward to eastern California, central Arizona, the southern tip of the Baja Peninsula, and southern Sinaloa, Mexico.

Northern Zebra-tailed Lizard
Callisaurus draconoides myurus

Western Zebra-tailed Lizard
Callisaurus draconoides rhodostictus

Eastern Zebra-tailed Lizard
Callisaurus d. ventralis

Habitat: This is a denizen of sparsely vegetated aridlands. It may be found on many substrates, including gravel, hardpan, stabilized sands, and even yielding sand. You may encounter this species at below sea level to about 5,000 feet in elevation.

Size: The zebra-tail reaches a maximum length of about 10 inches, but most examples are 7½–9 inches long. The tail is about 120% of the SVL.

Identifying features: A flattened but slender body, a flattened tail, very long limbs, and an upturned, wagging tail ringed with black will identify these lizards.

The back and sides may be a golden brown, tan, or of some shade of gravel gray. There are 2 black bars on the anterior lower sides. These wrap around onto the belly and on adult males connect to blue belly patches. There are obscure, darker dorsal bars or spots along the back as well as a liberal peppering of light spots. The tail is very conspicuously barred anteriorly and ringed distally. The throat is white with gray streaks and a red orange central area that distends into a fan during territorial displays. The limbs are very long. Except for the subspecies that is found on the Viscaino Desert of southern Baja, there are no fringes on the toes.

Similar species: Several species of earless lizard look superficially similar; however, all lack ear openings. Fringe-toed lizards have a fringe of scales along the toes on the hind feet.

Comments: True heliotherms, these desert speedsters (in short spurts the speed of a zebra-tail at optimal body temperature has been estimated at 15 mph!) remain in hiding in cloudy or foggy weather; however, as the sun warms the landscape, they will first bask for a half hour or so and then begin to actively forage. When too hot the lizards will lift their body away from the substrate, then tip their toes upward (standing only on the heel) and orient their nose toward the sun. Both instinctive ploys reduce the body surface being heated. Eventually they will seek the dappled shade of a desert shrub in which to rest.

ADDITIONAL SUBSPECIES

Attempting to differentiate the subspecies of this lizard can be an exercise in futility. It is largely based on comparative lengths of the tail and hind leg.

Northern zebra-tailed lizard. Photo by R. W. Van Devender

67. Northern Zebra-tailed Lizard, *Callisaurus draconoides myurus*: tail 57% or less of the total length; 91% of the body length or shorter; 16 or fewer femoral pores; northwestern Nevada.

68. Western Zebra-tailed Lizard, *Callisaurus draconoides rhodostictus*: tail 58% or more of the total length; 92% of the body length or longer; 16 or fewer femoral pores; southeastern California, western Arizona, to the southern tip of the Baja Peninsula.

Western zebra-tailed lizard

Eastern zebra-tailed lizard

69. The Eastern Zebra-tailed lizard, *Callisaurus draconoides ventralis*: tail 56% or less of the total length; 91% of the body length or shorter; 17 or more femoral pores; central Arizona southward to southern Sinaloa.

Earless Lizards, Genera *Cophosaurus* and *Holbrookia*

The common name of "earless" defines one of the primary identifying characteristics of these alert, fast moving lizards. They lack an ear opening. The earless lizards are of variable dorsal color, the hues usually closely matching those of the sands on which the lizards are found. A variable light dorsal and lateral speckling or flecking affords the lizards even greater camouflage.

Look for these lizards among low, sparse desert herbs and in pebbly terrain with occasional larger rocks on which the lizards will bask. In rural areas they may be seen along the edged of paved or sand roads, often atop low berms or curbstones, or on substrate-level cement culvert drains.

From 1 to 9 eggs are laid in each clutch and multiclutching may occur.

70. Chihuahuan Greater Earless Lizard

Cophosaurus texanus scitulus

Abundance/Range: This is a common lizard that blends well with its background. It occurs from the Big Bend and Trans-Pecos area westward to central Arizona. It also occurs in Mexico.

Habitat: This beautiful lizard is associated with rock fields, rocky flats, rocky washes, jumbled scree at the foot of escarpments, road cuts, and other such rock-strewn habitats.

Size: Adult males may attain a full 7 inches in total length. Females are smaller. These are flattened but stocky lizards with a tail slightly longer than the SVL. Hatchlings are about 2 inches long.

Identifying features: This lizard blends remarkably with the color of the boulders over which it scampers. The scales are smoothly granular. There are two skin folds across the throat. The dorsal coloration can be

Chihuahuan greater earless lizard

tan, brown, or gray, even reddish, and may change rather abruptly from a darker to a lighter (greenish or yellowish) color posterior to the dark lateral bars. Lighter lateral spots are present, and there may be indications of darker dorsal barring. The venter is white centrally. Females, especially when gravid, have an orange to peach wash ventrolaterally and laterally. A greenish or yellowish color can also be present laterally. Males have a field of bright blue crossed by two black bars posterio-ventrolaterally. Legs and toes are proportionately long. The underside of the tail is prominently barred with black. Vague darker bars are usually present on the dorsal surface of the tail and limbs. When the lizard is running, its tail may be curved upward, displaying the spots. This lizard stops abruptly after each short dash and, were it not for the easily seen spots on the underside of the waving tail, would then be lost to sight.

Similar species: The several races of the lesser earless lizard are smaller and less colorful, and they lack spots beneath the tail. Zebra-tailed lizards have spots beneath the tail and also have ear openings.

ADDITIONAL SUBSPECIES

None within the scope of this guide.

71. Lesser Earless Lizards

Holbrookia elegans ssp. and *H. maculata* ssp.

Taxonomic comment: Despite there being two species of small western earless lizards, we will mention both under this heading. The first, now known as the Sonoran earless lizard, *Holbrookia elegans thermophila*, was initially described as a subspecies of the wide-ranging *Holbrookia maculata*. In fact, it was separated from the latter merely because of a taxonomic technicality. The validity of at least some of the subspecies in accounts 71a through 71f is questionable.

Additional taxonomic confusion exists with some populations of the speckled earless lizard, *Holbrookia maculata approximans*, for which the names *H. m. campi* and *H. m. flavilenta* have been erected. We have elected herein to retain the use of *H. m. approximans* as it has been traditionally used.

Abundance/Range: Collectively, these are common to abundant lizards. The subspecies discussed here range westward from South Dakota and

Wyoming to Arizona. They also range deeply into Mexico. One subspecies is found east of the range of this guide.

Habitat: Sandy meadows, grasslands, gravelly washes, and roadside expanses of sand and gravel are all acceptable habitats to these lizards.

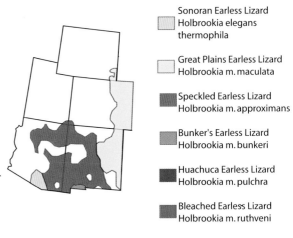

Sonoran Earless Lizard
Holbrookia elegans thermophila

Great Plains Earless Lizard
Holbrookia m. maculata

Speckled Earless Lizard
Holbrookia m. approximans

Bunker's Earless Lizard
Holbrookia m. bunkeri

Huachuca Earless Lizard
Holbrookia m. pulchra

Bleached Earless Lizard
Holbrookia m. ruthveni

Many may be seen basking on curbstones along rural roadways. Collectively, these lizards may be found from sea level to about 7,000 feet in elevation.

Size: The lizards in this group are aptly named. Most are adult at about 4¼ inches total length, and none exceed 5½ inches. The tail is about 120% of the SVL. The tiny hatchlings measure about 1½ inches in overall length.

Identifying features: These are small, slender, wary, and fast lizards. They have short tails that lack either rings or subcaudal spots. Most are clad in scales of a color that closely matches the substrate on which they live. The back may be tan to gray and has about 9 pairs of darker spots with a light posterior edge and a liberal peppering of tiny white dots. The dark dorsal spots are often less prominent on the males. Paired black spots on the lower sides and outer belly *may* be contained in small patches of pale blue. Gravid females have a suffusion of orange on the lower sides and an orange chin.

Similar species: Some of these subspecies are confusingly similar to others. Use range as a principal identification criterion. Check all designations in this account carefully.

SPECIES AND SUBSPECIES

71a. The Sonoran Earless Lizard, *Holbrookia elegans thermophila*, ranges southward to Sonora, Mexico, from central southern Arizona. The dark dorsal markings of the male are largely obscured by a liberal peppering of white dots. The female is less strongly spotted with white. The ventro-

Sonoran earless lizard

lateral bars are contained in blue. The tail is as long as, or slightly longer than, the SVL.

71b. The Great Plains Earless Lizard, *Holbrookia maculata maculata*, is a dark and rather prominently striped race. It is found from Texas to South Dakota and westward to southeastern Wyoming and eastern Colorado. The ground color may be so dark that the dorsal blotches (usually 2 rows on each side of the vertebral stripe) are all but obscured, or they may be rather well defined and at least partially edged with light pigment.

Great Plains earless lizard

A varying amount of faint white speckling is usually present. Vertebral, dorsolateral, and lateral stripes are present. The dorsolateral stripe separates the two rows of dark blotches on each side, and the lateral stripe defines the lowest limit of the dorsal coloration. The anterio-ventrolateral bars are prominent and encircled narrowly with blue (male), or they are tiny and not contained in blue (female). Females are apt to be paler dorsally than the males, but become suffused with yellowish, pink, or peach laterally when gravid.

71c. The Speckled Earless Lizard, *Holbrookia maculata approximans*, is a white-speckled race. It ranges westward from western Texas to Arizona and northward to Utah and Colorado. Like many lizards, these lizards are darker in color when cold and/or inactive. They are dimorphic, with males normally slightly larger and considerably lighter in color. A vertebral stripe is present. In this race, the dorsolateral stripes normally present on other subspecies are absent or visible only anteriorly. There are 7 (or more) paired dorsal blotches, often edged posteriorly with light pigment (sometimes quite obscure) from the nape to above the vent. There may be obscure lateral blotches alternating with the dorsal blotches. The dorsum is usually peppered with small light spots. Two short, anterio-ventrolateral black bars are narrowly encircled with blue. Although the black bars are present on the female, they are smaller, and she lacks the encircling blue. The female is darker, has smaller dorsal blotches and more contrasting lateral blotches, and becomes suffused with peach color when gravid. The tail is short, being no longer than the SVL.

Speckled earless lizard

Bunker's earless lizard

71d. Bunker's Earless Lizard, *Holbrookia maculata bunkeri*, ranges north-ward from Chihuahua, Mexico, into Dona Ana and Luna counties in south central New Mexico. This, another of the speckled earless lizards, is poorly known in the United States but supposedly differs genetically from the more common *H. m. approximans*.

71e. The Huachuca Earless Lizard, *Holbrookia maculata pulchra*, occurs at high elevations in the Huachuca Mountains of southeastern Arizona. Although males are speckled, the flecking is far less evident than in more

Huachuca earless lizard

easterly races. The dorsal blotches of the females may be well defined or rather obscure. The black ventrolateral bars are narrowly surrounded by blue.

71f. The Bleached Earless Lizard, *Holbrookia maculata ruthveni*, is restricted to the White Sands area of north central New Mexico. Females are the darker and more robust sex, but are still considerably lighter than females of the surrounding *H. m. approximans*. Males are an almost uniform, bleached white. The black ventrolateral markings are more anterior than in surrounding races, and they are not surrounded with blue. In fact, except for the intrusion of the black bars onto the belly, the belly is an immaculate white.

Bleached earless lizard

Rock Lizards, Genus *Petrosaurus*

This genus comprises three active diurnal species that are of primarily Mexican (Baja Peninsula) distribution. Only a single species, the banded rock lizard, occurs in the United States, and it is restricted to escarpments and boulder-strewn terrain in south central California.

72. Banded Rock Lizard

Petrosaurus mearnsi

Abundance/Range: This is a relatively common but very locally distributed lizard. It ranges southward from south central San Bernardino County, California, to well into Baja California.

Habitat: This lizard is restricted in distribution to areas of boulders and outcroppings in desert canyons. It is found from sea level to about 3,500 feet in elevation.

Size: The maximum size is about 12 inches in length. The long slender tail is about 180% (or more) of the SVL. Hatchlings are about 3 inches long.

Identifying features: This is a long-limbed lizard with a spraddle-legged stance and a rather distinctive waddling gait with the body held close against the rock. The body color is olive gray to slate gray (or darker if the lizard is cold). The dorsal scales are small and granular; those on the limbs and tail are keeled and sharply pointed. There is a single, light-edged black collar. There are about 5 dark bands across the dorsum from shoulders to tailbase. The tail is also prominently banded. The belly is grayish. Males have blue patches along the sides of the belly, and the throat is reticulated with dark gray on light.

Banded rock lizard

Similar species: The Baja collared lizard has 2 black collars, and both are usually broadly broken dorsally.

Comments: This lizard moves quickly and agilely over the tops, sides, and even bottoms of granitic boulders, all with equal facility. Besides insects, the rock lizard preys upon smaller lizards (such as tree lizards) that also occur on rock faces.

ADDITIONAL SUBSPECIES

None.

Horned Lizards, Genus *Phrynosoma*

These are the most unmistakable of the North American lizards. As a group all are flattened and all are spiny—but some are spinier than others—and all have short tails. The group is most diverse in Mexico and the western United States, with only a single small species reaching extreme southern Alberta and Saskatchewan, Canada.

Most lay eggs, but the two species of short-horned lizard give birth to live young.

A very unusual defensive ploy that is utilized by some species is to squirt a few drops of blood from the corner of the eye at an enemy. Dogs, whether or not possessed of malicious intent, seem capable of evoking this response from the horned lizards.

Most horned lizards (most often referred to by those who see them as horned toads or horny toads) feed largely on ants. Several species of these lizards seem to prefer the black harvester ants, but at least one species snacks contentedly on honey-pot ants.

These are all small lizards. The largest species in the United States reaches only 6½ inches in total length and the smallest species is about half of that length.

They are diurnal heliotherms, but may occasionally be found on roadways at night. All blend well with the substrates on which they are found, and some rely so strongly on the effectiveness of their camouflaging colors and patterns that they will lie still and allow themselves to be picked up. A certain amount of metachrosis (literally "change" + "color") is possible, with an individual lizard being dark at one time and light at another.

Mode of reproduction varies. The greater short-horned lizards and the pygmy short-horned lizards give birth to 5–50 living young. The remain-

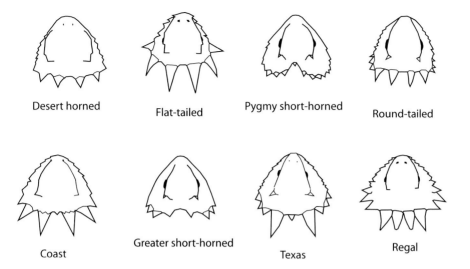

Desert horned
Flat-tailed
Pygmy short-horned
Round-tailed

Coast
Greater short-horned
Texas
Regal

Horned lizard heads showing horn arrangements

ing species within our area of coverage lay eggs. Varying by species, between 5 and 50 eggs are laid in a clutch.

73. Coast Horned Lizard

Phrynosoma blainvillii

Abundance/Range: Land development is taking its toll on the populations of this pretty horned lizard. Although actual population statistics are still lacking, this species has been extirpated or seriously reduced over vast areas where it was once common. It is found from north central California southward to northern Baja California.

Habitat: Look for this lizard in sandy areas of open coastal or inland scrub. It is also found in grasslands and open woodland at altitudes up to 8,000 feet. It may occasionally be seen basking on the edges of paved roads in the early morning or late afternoon.

Size: This is a large horned lizard. Although most examples are between 4½ and 6 inches in total length, they occasionally reach a full 7 inches long. The tail is a little less than one-third the SVL. Hatchlings are about 1¼ inches long.

Coast horned lizard

Identifying features: This is a reddish, tan, or buff lizard dorsally. The venter is white. The nape blotches are very large and prominent. Posterior to the large nape blotches, to a point above the vent, there are four pairs of broad, irregular bars (each bar may be divided into 2 spots) with light posterior edges. There is a light, but not always well-defined, vertebral stripe. There are 2 rows of large fringe scales. There are 2 or 3 rows of serrate scales on each side of the throat. When frightened, this lizard may inflate itself prodigiously. The two center horns are noticeably elongated but do not touch at the base.

Similar species: The desert horned lizard has one row of enlarged throat scales, and these are comparatively small. Although two rows of lateral fringe scales are present, only the upper row is noticeably enlarged.

Comments: This is another of the horned lizards that can eject a stream of blood from the corner of the eye and direct it toward a predator.

ADDITIONAL SUBSPECIES

As currently understood, none.

74. Texas Horned Lizard

Phrynosoma cornutum

Abundance/Range: Populations of this intriguing lizard, long thought to be on the decline, may be stabilizing in some areas. Actual population statistics remain unknown. The Texas horned lizard ranges from western Louisiana and Missouri to southeastern Arizona and deeply into Mexico.

Habitat: Look for this lizard in sandy areas of grasslands and prairies, in sandy fields, dunes, and areas of open scrub. It often basks on the edges of paved roads in the early morning or late afternoon.

Size: Most specimens of the Texas horned lizard range between 3½ and 6 inches in total length. The tail is a little less than one-third the SVL. Hatchlings are about 1¼ inches long.

Identifying features: This is a reddish, tan, or buff lizard dorsally. The venter is white. Posterior to the large nape blotches, to a point above the vent, there are 4 pairs of light-edged, irregular, dark spots on each side of the light vertebral line. Normally this is a flattened lizard (that looks more streamlined when it folds its ribs back to dart through grasses); however, when frightened it may inflate itself prodigiously. The two center horns are noticeably elongated.

Texas horned lizard

Similar species: The round-tailed horned lizard is smaller, less spinous overall, lacks fringe scales, and has all 4 major horns of about equal length. The greater short-horned lizard has 4 very short horns of equal length. The regal horned lizard has 4 very long horns of similar size and with the bases touching.

Comments: When seriously frightened, the Texas horned lizard may squirt a stream of blood toward the disturbing object from the corner of its eye. It sinks beneath the surface of loose sand by flattening its body and using a side to side shuffling motion. It may then sit quietly with only its eyes, horns, and nostrils visible, or go entirely beneath the sand.

75. Pygmy Short-horned Lizard

Phrynosoma douglasii

Abundance/Range: This horned lizard is common but secretive and so well camouflaged that it is often overlooked. It is found in Washington, Oregon, Idaho, and extreme northern California and Nevada.

Habitat: Look for this lizard in open brushlands and woodlands, often near grass clumps and rocks, at elevations between 1,000 and 6,000 feet.

Size: This short-horned species is adult at 3½–4¼ inches in total length. Of this, the tail is about 1½ inches long. Neonates are about 1 inch long.

Coloration/pattern: Some degree of color change is possible. This species is darkest when cold. The dorsal coloration of this lizard usually closely matches the color of the soil and rocks on which it dwells and may be tan to reddish or reddish brown. There is a light vertebral stripe, and a single row of small lateral fringe scales. There may be up to 7 pairs of dark paravertebral spots with light-colored posterior edges. A prominent dark nape blotch is present. The tail is banded. The belly is yellow or reddish, often with considerable dark pigment.

Similar species: No other horned lizard occurs within the range of this species.

Top: Pygmy short-horned lizard, adult. Photo by R. W. Van Devender

Above: Pygmy horned lizards, neonates

Left: Intermediate between pygmy and greater short-horned lizard, northern Nevada

76. Greater Short-horned Lizard

Phrynosoma hernandesi

Abundance/Range: This pretty horned lizard is quiet and easily overlooked. It occurs from the Davis and Guadalupe Mountains of Texas northward and westward to western Arizona, northwestern Nevada, and southeastern Alberta.

Habitat: The greater short-horned lizard is associated with sparsely wooded grasslands, shrubby deserts, and clearings in mountain fastnesses. It ranges upward from about 1,000 feet to more than 11,000 feet in elevation.

Size: With a record length of 6⁵⁄₁₆ inches, this is one of the larger horned lizards. Most specimens are between 3½ and 5 inches in total length. Neonates are about 1¼ inches long.

Identifying features: Some degree of color change is possible. This species is darkest when cold. The dorsal coloration of this lizard usually closely matches the color of the soil and rocks on which it dwells and may be tan

Greater short-horned lizard

to reddish or reddish brown, often with highlights of orange or yellow. It is often darkest along a poorly defined vertebral line and just above the orange(ish) area that borders the white lateral fringe scales dorsally. A prominent dark nape blotch is present, as are three other dark blotches posterior to the nape blotch. The tail is banded. The belly is yellow or reddish, often with considerable dark pigment.

Similar species: The pygmy horned lizard is smaller and has mere nubbins for horns.

Comments: If molested unduly, the greater short-horned lizard may lower its head and attempt to butt or approach the offending object and attempt to bite. This lizard is also one of the several species in this genus that is able to squirt blood toward a predator from the corner of its eye.

Like its congeners, it eats a goodly proportion of harvester ants.

Large females of this live-bearing lizard can produce surprisingly large clutches. Although most clutches seem to number 6–17 babies, up to 31 have been recorded. The babies are born in a nearly transparent amniotic sac from which they must soon escape. Gestation averages about 80 days.

77. Flat-tailed Horned Lizard

Phrynosoma mcallii

Abundance/Range: This is an uncommon to rare horned lizard throughout its range. Its populations have been impacted adversely by agriculture and off-road vehicles. It is found in southeastern California, southwestern Arizona, and extreme northwestern Sonora, Mexico.

Habitat: This is a species of gravelly deserts and hardpan habitats. It utilizes loose sand for burrowing. This is a low-elevation species.

Size: This uncommon horned lizard is adult at 3–5 inches in total length. The very flat tail is about 60% of the SVL. Hatchlings are about 1¼ inches long.

Identifying features: A single feature will positively identify this horned lizard: it has a *dark* vertebral stripe. The dorsal color of tan, buff, or grayish almost perfectly matches the substrate on which the lizard is found. The horns are slender and thin, and the two center ones are the longest. The

Flat-tailed horned lizard

posterior temporal horn curves rearward. The horns are often brighter than the lizard's skin. The nape blotches are present but are not usually well defined. There are 3 or 4 pairs of double spots along the length of the back and each surrounds a spine. There are 2 rows of lateral fringe scales. The belly is white.

Similar species: None. All other horned lizards have light vertebral stripes.

Comments: This horned lizard relies on its camouflaging color to protect it from harm. It will often remain in place with head bowed and eyes closed and allow itself to be picked up. When on a road it flattens so much that little shadow is thrown, making it very difficult to see.

ADDITIONAL SUBSPECIES

None.

78. Round-tailed Horned Lizard

Phrynosoma modestum

Abundance/Range: Although this lizard is easily overlooked because of its skulking habits, it is not an uncommon species. We recently found more than 20 within 15 minutes as they basked in the waning rays

Round-tailed horned lizard

Round-tailed horned lizards

of the evening sun on a paved roadway in Texas' western Big Bend. The round-tailed horned lizard occurs in suitable habitats over the western half of Texas, and from there westward to southeastern Arizona and far southward into Mexico.

Habitat: Arid plains and grasslands and open shrubby desert are home to this interesting, small horned lizard.

Size: This is the smallest horned lizard of the west. It is adult at 3–3¼ inches in total length. The record size is a mere 4⅛ inches. Hatchlings are only about 1 inch long.

Identifying features: The round-tailed horned lizard is capable of considerable color change, not only from dark when cold to light when hot, but also to an entirely different color and pattern. The color may vary from dust gray to red, and the pattern may vary from virtually absent to prominent. The posterior horns are moderately prominent and of about the same length as the temporal horns. The body lacks a fringe of enlarged lateral scales. The round tail narrows abruptly posterior to the vent.

Similar species: The short-horned lizards have very short horns and a prominent lateral fringe of scales. The Texas horned lizard has the two central horns much longer than all flanking horns and also has a prominent lateral fringe.

Comments: This strange little lizard has the disconcerting habit of lying tightly against the substrate, body flattened and throwing no shadow, until the last possible moment before running. When on a desert flat, this behavior can be startling to the observer, but it can also be harmful to the lizard, which can be stepped on. The lizard also uses this ploy on dusty desert roads, where it is then frequently run over. Once routed, the lizard makes a short dash, then abruptly stops, again blending perfectly with the dusty substrate.

This, the smallest and most easily overlooked of our horned lizards, will, if prodded, arch its back (like a frightened cat), press its head tightly against the substrate, close its eyes, and remain still.

ADDITIONAL SUBSPECIES

None.

79. Northern Desert Horned Lizard

Phrynosoma platyrhinos platyrhinos

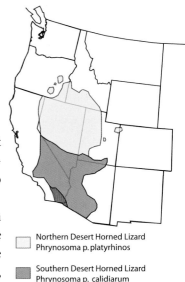

Abundance/Range: This is an abundant horned lizard. It is found from central western Oregon and adjacent Idaho southward to southern Nevada and southern Utah.

Habitat: This horned lizard is found in a wide range of habitats. It may be on fine wind-blown sand, gravel, or hard pan. There is usually sagebrush, creosote, greasewood, or other desert plants present for cover. This lizard often sits on rocks or dirt clods to ther-

Northern Desert Horned Lizard
Phrynosoma p. platyrhinos

Southern Desert Horned Lizard
Phrynosoma p. calidiarum

Goode's Desert Horned Lizard
Phrynosoma p. goodei

Northern desert horned lizard

moregulate. It is found from below sea level in washes and valleys to about 6,500 feet in elevation.

Size: The largest authenticated size is about 5½ inches. The tail is only 40% of the SVL. Hatchlings are about 1¼ inches long.

Identifying features: There is a single row of lateral fringe scales and the single row of chin shields is only modestly enlarged. The horns are moderately developed, with the longest 2 being 45% or less of the head length and the space between them about equal to the width of the horn base. The dorsum usually blends well with whatever substrate the lizard is on, be it gray, black (lava), red, white, or tan. There are 3 or 4 poorly defined dark blotches or spots on each side of the back. The belly is white with scattered dark scales.

Similar species: No other horned lizard has only a single row of enlarged chin shields and a single row of lateral fringe scales.

ADDITIONAL SUBSPECIES

80. The Southern Desert Horned Lizard, *Phrynosoma platyrhinos calidiarum,* ranges southward from southern Nevada and Utah to eastern Baja California and northwestern Sonora, Mexico. The longest 2 horns are 45% of the head length or longer. The space between the 2 horns is less than half the width of the horn base.

Southern desert horned lizard

81. Goode's Desert Horned Lizard, *Phrynosoma platyrhinos goodei*, is considered a full species by some authorities. It is identical in appearance to the southern desert horned lizard, but differs in DNA structure. It is found in the Salton Trough.

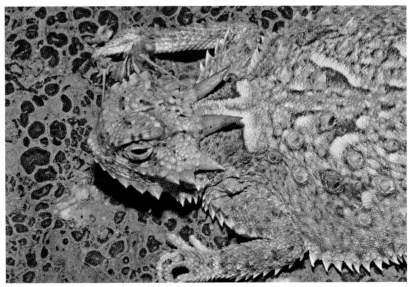

Goode's desert horned lizard

82. Regal Horned Lizard
Phrynosoma solare

Abundance/Range: This is a relatively common horned lizard species. It is found southward from southern Arizona to southern Sinaloa, Mexico.

Habitat: The regal horned lizard prefers gravelly desert habitats with plant associations of saguaro, ocotillo, and mesquite. It is often found amid areas of succulent plant growth. It may be found from sea level to about 5,000 feet in elevation.

Size: This is marginally our largest horned lizard species. The adult size may be up to 6½ inches in total length. The tail is only about one-third of the SVL. Hatchlings are about 1½ inches long.

Identifying features: This is a large horned lizard with a very short tail. The color is variable, but the outer perimeter of the back is darker than the center. The delineation between the two colors is perceptibly abrupt. The back may be tan, gray, buff, or reddish. There may or may not be a light vertebral stripe. Nape blotches are present but are not well defined, especially posteriorly. The belly is dirty white with scattered gray scales. There is just one row of lateral fringe scales.

Similar species: None. No other horned lizard has the crown of 4 large horns with their bases all touching.

Regal horned lizard

ADDITIONAL SUBSPECIES

None.

Sagebrush and Bunchgrass Lizards

The spiny lizards in this group are all of small size. Although all can climb, none are truly arboreal. All are oviparous, females laying from one to several clutches annually.

83. Dunes Sagebrush Lizard

Sceloporus arenicolus

Abundance/Range: This lizard is fairly common, but is of very localized distribution. It occurs only in the vicinity of the Monahans Sandhills region of Texas and near Roswell, New Mexico.
Habitat: This is a specialized lizard that occupies only active and semistabilized dunes. Growth of dwarf shin oaks and sagebrush is prevalent in these habitats.
Size: This is a moderately sized spiny lizard. It is adult at 5–6 inches in

Dunes sagebrush lizard

total length. The tail is slightly greater in length than the SVL. Hatchlings are about 1¾ inches in total length.

Identifying features: The pale tan to pale buff dorsal coloration of this lizard is as pale as the sands of its dunes home. There is a broad dorsolateral stripe on each side that is conspicuously paler than the dorsum. Lateral surfaces are also very light in color. Males have a blue ventrolateral patch on each side. Each patch is bordered along its inner length by deeper blue or black. The remaining part of the male's venter and the venter of the female is nearly white. The outer areas of the throat and the lower sides of an ovulating or a gravid female are flushed with orange. The scales on the posterior of each thigh are granular and nonspinous. There may be a dark spot anterior to each forelimb.

Similar species: Other species of spiny lizard have spiny scales on the rear of each thigh. Side-blotched lizards have a dark spot posterior to each forelimb.

Comments: This lizard is protected by state law, and is currently a candidate for federal protection as well.

84. Northern Sagebrush Lizard

Sceloporus graciosus graciosus

Abundance/Range: This is a common lizard throughout its vast range. It is found from northern Washington to eastern California and then eastward to New Mexico and North Dakota.

Habitat: Although often associated with sagebrush habitats, this lizard is also found on rock faces and stumps in other plant associations as well as in pine-oak woodlands at quite considerable elevations. It ranges in elevation from about 500 feet to more than 10,000 feet.

Size: This is a moderately sized spiny lizard. It is adult at 5–6 inches in total length. The tail is slightly greater in length than the SVL. Hatchlings are about 1¾ inches in total length.

Northern Sagebrush Lizard, *Sceloporus g. graciosus*

Western Sagebrush Lizard, *Sceloporus g. gracilis*

Southern Sagebrush Lizard, *Sceloporus g. vandenburghianus*

Northern sagebrush lizard

Identifying features: This is a very typical "fence lizard" in overall appearance, but it does have some features that make identification rather easy. The dorsal color can vary from light to dark gray or brown, but is often quite dark, especially if the lizard is disturbed. There are about 10 pairs of irregular darker spots on the back. There are also dark spots on the sides. There are 4 stripes—2 dorsolateral and 2 lateral. These may be poorly defined. The dorsal and lateral scales are quite small but are spiny. The scales on the back of the thighs are granular and nonspinose. There may be scattered blue scales on the back and on the sides of the tail. The apices of the limbs are often rusty. The males have a pale blue throat and bright blue belly patches that are edged with black on their inner edges. The chest is often dusky. Females are smaller and lack most or all of the blue.

Similar species: Other spiny lizards in our area of coverage have spiny scales on the rear of the thighs.

ADDITIONAL SUBSPECIES

85. The Western Sagebrush Lizard, *Sceloporus graciosus gracilis*, is the sagebrush lizard race of southern Oregon to central California.

Rely on range to identify this race. It is very much like the northern sagebrush lizard but has smaller scales, thus a greater number of scale rows along the length of the back. The stripes are usually very poorly defined.

Western sagebrush lizard

86. The Southern Sagebrush Lizard, *Sceloporus graciosus vandenburgianus*, is found in southern California and northern Baja California. It tends to have more blue on the belly and throat than the other races. Again, we urge that you rely primarily on range to identify this sagebrush lizard.

Southern sagebrush lizard

87. Slevin's Bunchgrass Lizard

Sceloporus sleveni

Abundance/Range: Where found, this can be a fairly common lizard; however, in the United States its range is spotty and quite restricted. It is found in southeastern Arizona, adjacent southwestern New Mexico, and northern Mexico.

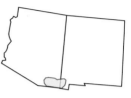

Habitat: In the United States this taxon is found in relatively high bunchgrass habitats. It is most common at elevations between 4,000 and 6,500 feet; however, in Mexico it has been found at up to 11,000 feet in elevation.

Size: This is a small sceloporine, fully grown at about 4 inches in total length. The tail is about half of the length. Neonates are about 1¾ inches long.

Identifying features: The rows of scales on the sides parallel those on the back. They are not in diagonal rows like those of other species in this group.

This is a sexually dimorphic species. Males tend to be quite pallid. The back is light gray, with or without about 13 pairs of brownish, rearward-directed chevrons. The dorsal color is separated from the tan sides by a

Slevin's bunchgrass lizard, male

Slevin's bunchgrass lizard, female

light yellow to orangish dorsolateral stripe. Males usually have blue belly patches.

Females are brownish with gray vertebral stripes and tan dorsolateral stripes. There are about a dozen pairs of rearward-directed chevrons on the back; these are edged with black posteriorly. A row of chevrons is also present below each dorsolateral stripe. The belly is light and usually lacks blue.

Similar species: The striped plateau lizard has 4 prominent stripes and diagonal rows of scales on each side.

ADDITIONAL SUBSPECIES

As now understood, none.

Spiny Lizards, Fence Lizards, and Swifts

Taxonomic uncertainty is rampant in this lizard group. The subspecies of several species, among them the Sonoran spiny lizard, the desert spiny lizard (the term used for all subspecies of *S. magister* when discussed collectively), and the western fence lizard, are of questionable validity as now described.

The majority of the lizards in this group are very spiny. The differentiating characteristics between many of the species are subtle, easily overlooked unless the specimen is in hand, and even then, some are very obscure and confusing.

In many cases the geographic location where the lizard was seen may help more with a positive identification than the creature's appearance.

The species in this group vary in size from the 5¾-inch prairie lizard to the heavy-bodied 13-inch Sonoran spiny lizard. Reproductively active females may produce eggs or give live birth. Egg-layers often have more than one clutch a season, while those that birth live young produce only a single clutch each year.

Most of the species are clad in scales that blend well in color and pattern with the rocks and trees on which they live. Only one, the granite spiny lizard, could be considered truly colorful.

Most spiny lizards, and especially the adult males, are very wary and will not allow close approach by a human. They are easiest to approach soon after they emerge from their nighttime hiding areas, before they have fully heated up for the day's activities.

Most are insectivorous, but some will eat berries, blossoms, and pollen.

88. Sonoran Spiny Lizard

Sceloporus clarkii clarkii

Abundance/Range: This is a rather common but difficult to see spiny lizard. It is found from northwestern Arizona to southwestern New Mexico and then southward deeply into Mexico.

Sonoran Spiny Lizard, Sceloporus c. clarkii

[x] Plateau Spiny Lizard, Sceloporus c. vallaris

Habitat: Although principally a species of the trees, Sonoran spiny lizards also may be seen amid rocks and on escarpments. When near humans they may become fence and wall dwellers. They range from sea level to near 6,000 feet in elevation.

Size: Although adult at 8–10 inches in length, occasional males may attain a total length of 13 inches. The tail is about 125% of the SVL. Hatchlings are about 3 inches in length.

Sonoran spiny lizard

Identifying features: This is normally a gray, bluish gray, or greenish lizard, but it can be nearly black when cold and inactive or when badly stressed. Dorsal banding is usually prominent. Shoulder wedges are present. This species has banded forearms. Males have blue belly patches and a blue throat patch. The body and tail scales are very spiny. Juveniles are very strongly banded on both body and tail.

Similar species: The subspecies of the desert spiny lizard lack banding on the forearms and are more tan or brown in color. Western fence lizards lack the shoulder wedges.

Comments: If unused to humans, this is a very wary species. The most usual ploy is to squirrel around the tree or rock on which it is sitting, keeping that object between it and the approaching person.

ADDITIONAL SUBSPECIES

89. The Plateau Spiny Lizard, *Sceloporus clarkii vallaris*, of Yavapai County, Arizona, is of very questionable validity. Its only supposed difference is retention of the strongly contrasting pattern of the juveniles throughout its life.

Plateau spiny lizard

90. Mountain Spiny Lizard

Sceloporus jarrovii

Abundance/Range: This is another Mexican species that ranges northward to southeastern Arizona. It is fairly common at high altitudes in several of the mountain ranges. Among these are the Dos Cabezas, the Dragoon, the Huachucas, the Chiricahuas and other nearby ranges.

Habitat: This is a rock-dwelling lizard found in talus and on escarpments from 4,500 feet to more than 11,000 feet in elevation.

Size: Adults often attain 7 inches in total length and may occasionally reach 8½ inches. The tail is about 130% of the SVL. Neonates are about 2 inches long.

Identifying features: This is a pretty spiny lizard. The slate gray, blue gray, or pinkish scales have black edging, producing an overall tracery of black on the back and sides. A broad black collar is edged posteriorly with white. The top of the head is very dark. There is a poorly defined light eye

Mountain spiny lizard

stripe and an equally poorly defined light jaw stripe. Males have blue belly patches and a blue throat. Neonates are paler than the adults.

Similar species: None. No other spiny lizard within our scope of coverage has the lace pattern produced by the dark-edged scales.

ADDITIONAL SUBSPECIES

None in the United States.

91–95. Desert Spiny Lizards

Sceloporus magister ssp.

91. Purple-backed Spiny Lizard

Sceloporus magister magister

Abundance/Range: This is a big, pretty, and common lizard. It is found from southwestern Arizona into Mexico.

Habitat: Although an agile climber, this spiny lizard is often found close to or actually on the ground. Look for it beneath cacti and succulents or in boulder fields or other rock-strewn areas. It often surveys its domain from the tops of roadside rocks.

Size: This is not only a large lizard, but a stocky one as well. It is adult

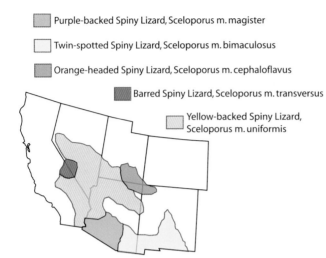

Purple-backed Spiny Lizard, Sceloporus m. magister

Twin-spotted Spiny Lizard, Sceloporus m. bimaculosus

Orange-headed Spiny Lizard, Sceloporus m. cephaloflavus

Barred Spiny Lizard, Sceloporus m. transversus

Yellow-backed Spiny Lizard,
Sceloporus m. uniformis

at 8–10 inches in total length. Occasional large males may attain 12 inches in length. Females seldom exceed 10 inches. The tail is 130% (or more) of the SVL. Hatchlings are about 3 inches in total length.

Identifying features: This normally tannish or brown lizard has blue and gold spangles on the sides, a purple back, and a bluish tail. The purple of the back is separated from the lateral color by a poorly defined yellowish stripe. Males have blue belly patches and a blue throat. A black wedge extends upward from the throat onto each

Purple-backed spiny lizard

shoulder. The limbs are bluish gray. Females are duller than the males, and juveniles are duller yet.

Similar species: None within the range of this species.

Comments: Whether or not the various subspecies are valid is controversial. Displaying males develop intense colors, bob their heads, and flex and extend their forelimbs in a series of push-ups. When on boulders, frightened lizards may seek refuge in holes beneath them. When in the trees, they "squirrel" noisily around large limbs and trunks, keeping the perch between them and the observer. At times these lizards (especially the large males) are wary and will seek safety while an observer is still a very long distance away. At other times they will allow rather close approach.

ADDITIONAL SUBSPECIES

92. The Twin-spotted Spiny Lizard, *Sceloporus magister bimaculosus*, is the easternmost race of this species. It is found from west Texas to central Arizona and southward into Mexico. This lizard is common near derelict buildings, in mesquite scrublands, on boulder-strewn hillsides grown to scrub and cactus, and in other similar habitats. Males have a tan or gray ground color and paired dark dorsal spots but may develop a blue suffu-

Twin-spotted spiny lizard

Twin-spotted spiny lizard, belly

sion of color on their back that is brightest during the breeding season. Isolated lateral scales may be yellow to peach in color. Males have blue belly patches and a blue throat patch. Some large, dominant males can be very intensely colored. The black shoulder wedge is apparent at all ages and on both sexes. Females and young are less colorful.

93. Both sexes of the Orange-headed Spiny Lizard, *Sceloporus magister cephaloflavus*, have a yellow to orangish head, but that of the male is brightest during the breeding season. There are 6 or 7 dark chevrons on the back. Males have blue belly patches and a blue patch on the throat. This is the race in the vicinity of the Four Corners.

Orange-headed spiny lizard

94. The Barred Spiny Lizard, *Sceloporus magister transversus*, is one of the least colorful races. It is olive brown to yellowish with about a half dozen darker dorsal crossbars. Males have blue belly patches and a blue throat patch. The shoulder wedge is prominent and extends well up onto the neck. This race occurs in eastern central California and immediately adjacent Nevada.

Barred spiny lizard

95. The Yellow-backed Spiny Lizard, *Sceloporus magister uniformis*, has a wide range in eastern California, Nevada, southwestern Utah, and northwestern Arizona. Males have a yellowish back, and the dorsal blotching is usually obscure. Males have a blue throat patch and blue belly patches. The shoulder wedge is prominent.

Yellow-backed spiny lizard

96–101. Western Fence Lizards

Sceloporus occidentalis ssp.

Abundance/Range: All of the 5 subspecies are common to abundant throughout most of their range. Collectively, the range encompasses the vast area between northern Washingon and northern Baja eastward to central Idaho and western Utah.

Habitat: These may be found from backyard habitats to the edges of mountain meadows. They may be seen on fences, rocks, building rubble, trash heaps, fallen trees, and other varied prominences.

Size: This species is adult at 5½–9½ inches in total length. The tail is about 150% of the SVL. Hatchlings are about 2¾ inches long.

Identifying features: This is a brown to grayish brown to almost black lizard with 6–8 pairs of dark markings with light posterior margins on the back. Sleeping, cold, or otherwise inactive lizards are the darkest. A light lateral line may be present. There may be scattered blue scales on the back, sides, and sides of the tail. Males have a blue throat and black-edged blue belly patches.

Similar species: The range of the eastern fence lizard does not overlap that of the western species. Sagebrush lizards lack keeled scales on the rear of the thigh and often have a black shoulder spot.

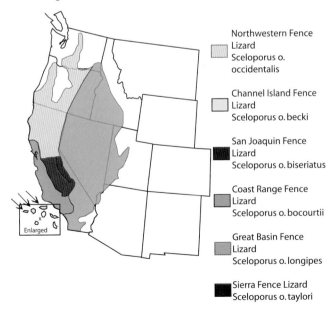

Northwestern Fence Lizard
Sceloporus o. occidentalis

Channel Island Fence Lizard
Sceloporus o. becki

San Joaquin Fence Lizard
Sceloporus o. biseriatus

Coast Range Fence Lizard
Sceloporus o. bocourtii

Great Basin Fence Lizard
Sceloporus o. longipes

Sierra Fence Lizard
Sceloporus o. taylori

Comments: The validity of at least some of the subspecies is questioned by some authorities.

ADDITIONAL SUBSPECIES

96. The Northwestern Fence Lizard, *Sceloporus occidentalis occidentalis*, ranges northward from central western California to northern Washington. This race has a dark blue chin patch on each side with either dark flecked white or blue between.

Northwestern fence lizard

97. Range alone will identify the Island Fence Lizard, *Sceloporus occidentalis becki*, of the Channel Islands. It has a very dark blue to black throat patch.

Island fence lizard

San Joaquin fence lizard

98. Save for the blue patches, the San Joaquin Fence Lizard, *Sceloporus occidentalis biseriatus*, of the lower San Joaquin Valley has a dark (sometimes almost black) belly. There is just a single blue throat patch.

99. Male Coast Range Fence Lizards, *Sceloporus occidentalis bocourtii*, have 2 small throat patches. They are found from San Mateo to Santa Barbara counties, California.

Coast Range fence lizard

Great Basin fence lizard

100. The Great Basin Fence Lizard, *Sceloporus occidentalis longipes*, is found from eastern Washington to southern Nevada, from eastern California to central Utah, and from southern California to northern Baja California. It has a single blue throat patch, blue belly patches, and a very dark belly.

101. Sierra Fence Lizard, *Sceloporus occidentalis taylori*, is found in the High Sierras. It can be quite dark dorsally, and the blue belly patches usually touch centrally.

Sierra fence lizard

102. Granite Spiny Lizard

Sceloporus orcutti

Abundance/Range: Although they can be present in sizable populations, granite spiny lizards are of localized occurrence. They range southward from southwestern California to the southern Baja Peninsula.

Habitat: This spiny lizard is associated with boulder fields, outcrops, and escarpments, but may occasionally be seen in construction rubble. It may be found from sea level to about 7,000 feet in elevation.

Size: This heavy-bodied lizard is adult at 8–10½ inches in length. Females are the smaller sex. The tail is about 150% of the SVL, but is often stubbed. The neonates are about 2¼ inches in total length.

Identifying features: This is a pretty but very variable lizard. It may be an olive green, rather bright green, or almost black. When dark, the ground color obscures the dark dorsal banding and the dark wedges on the shoulders. When the ground color is light, the darker markings often show up well. Adult males may have a deep purple back. The limbs and tail may be blue or bluish. The tail is obscurely banded and spiny. The scales of the back and sides are keeled but do not have a prominently projecting

Granite spiny lizard, dark phase

Granite spiny lizard, pair, light phase

spine on each. Males may have the entire belly a dark but shining blue. They also have a blue throat. Females are duller. Young may be brownish or grayish.

Similar species: The various races of the desert spiny lizard all have much spinier dorsal scales.

Comments: This is a wary lizard. The adults quickly scuttle to the far side of a boulder, or dart beneath it, when approached. The babies are usually less wary and may be approached to within a few feet. The babies often disperse to the periphery of a given habitat and remain close to the ground. They are, therefore, often more easily seen than the adults.

ADDITIONAL SUBSPECIES

None.

103. Crevice Spiny Lizard

Sceloporus poinsettii poinsettii

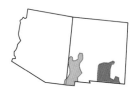

Crevice Spiny Lizard
Sceloporus p. poinsettii

Texas Crevice Spiny Lizard
Sceloporus p. axtelli

Abundance/Range: In suitable habitat, this can be a common species, but it is so alert and retiring that it is seldom seen. It is found from central Texas to southwestern New Mexico and from there southward to points well south of the international boundary.

Crevice spiny lizard

Habitat: Outcroppings, rocky road cuts, and mountain escarpments, where exfoliations, fissures, and crevices are plentiful, are the preferred habitats of this lizard. Habitats may be nearly devoid of vegetation or cloaked with trees and herbs. Crevice spiny lizards occur from an altitude of about 1,000 feet to as high as 8,400 feet.

Size: Large adult males of this heavy-bodied lizard may exceed 10 inches in total length. The record size is 11½ inches. Females are noticeably smaller. The original tail is about 135% of the SVL; however, large specimens often have stubbed-tails that are proportionately shorter. Neonates of this live-bearing species are about 2¾ inches long.

Identifying features: This is a very spiny species. The dorsal coloration of this large lizard varies from olive green to an olivey orangish, depending largely on the color of the rocks amid which it lives. The broad black collar is offset both anteriorly and posteriorly with a poorly defined light edging field. There are several poorly defined, but broad, dorsal crossbands. The tail is prominently banded along the distal two-thirds. Males have large, bright blue, ventrolateral patches that are bordered on their inner edges with black. The throat is also bright blue. Females have a grayish (sometimes speckled) throat and usually light ventral areas. Some females have very pale blue ventrolateral patches, but these lack black borders. Neonates are similarly colored, but the dorsal banding is more precisely delineated. Some neonates also have a dark vertebral stripe.

Similar species: The various races of the desert spiny lizard (see accounts 91–95) have black wedges on the throat rather than a well-defined collar.

Comments: This is an alert lizard that has usually sought shelter long before an observer has neared the spot where the lizard was last seen. Crevice spiny lizards are very appropriately named. They dart quickly behind rock exfoliations and into narrow escarpment fissures and crevices from which, because of their projecting spiny scales, the lizards are difficult to remove. It was learned during a lengthy study that only about 5% of the babies survive to breeding age, and considerably fewer survive to breed a second or third time.

ADDITIONAL SUBSPECIES

104. Based upon genetic differences, the crevice spiny lizards of Texas are now classified as *Sceloporus poinsettii axtelli*. The common name of Texas Crevice Spiny Lizard is now applied to these Texas populations. Use range as an identifying criterion.

Other subspecies are found in Mexico.

Texas crevice spiny lizard

Eastern Fence Lizard Group: Prairie Lizards and Plateau Lizards

Unlike the eastern members of this group, typified by chevron-shaped dorsal markings, the central and western forms have well-defined to obscure but visible light dorsolateral stripes.

Until recently, all of the species and subspecies listed in accounts 105–107 were considered divergent subspecies of the eastern fence lizard, *Sceloporus undulatus*. However, recent DNA analysis of the various forms divulged differences sufficient to prompt a complete revision of the species group. *Sceloporus undulatus* was divided into four species: *S. consobrinus*, *S. cowlesi*, *S. tristichus*, and *S. undulatus* (the last now extralimital to this guide). Into these four species, all other previous subspecies have been synonymized. As time has passed this concept seems to have gained additional endorsement and has been adopted here.

105. Prairie Lizard

Sceloporus consobrinus

Abundance/Range: This common lizard ranges westward from Texas to southeastern Arizona, northward to southeastern Wyoming and southwestern Idaho, and southward into Mexico.

Habitat: The prairie lizard is primarily terrestrial. It may be found in open, semidesert scrubland, in grasslands, on rocky hillsides, occasionally on rocky outcrops, or low in aridland shrubs.

Size: Typically, adults measure about 3½–6 inches. Males may occasionally attain 7 inches in total length. The tail is about 150% of the SVL. Hatchlings are about 1¾ inches in total length.

Identifying features: The dorsal scales are spiny, but not prominently large. This lizard bears dark dorsal markings in the form of 2 rows of spots that are often light edged posteriorly. The most prominent markings are the broad light dorsolateral stripes. A vertebral stripe, often gray in color, is usually strongly evident. Lateral stripes are present but may be largely obscured. The dorsal ground color is gray to olive tan or reddish brown. The sides are often somewhat brighter than the back. Males have black-

Prairie lizard (southern form)

Prairie lizard (northern form)

Prairie lizard (Mescalero Sands form)

edged blue ventrolateral patches. The remaining part of the venter is grayish. Males may also have a small black-bordered blue patch on each side of the throat (these may be lacking, which is rare) or so enlarged that they fuse across the middle of the throat). Females usually lack the blue ventrolateral and throat markings, but on some the blue may be palely evident. Gravid females may have orange on the sides of the jaw and develop more brilliant dorsal and lateral colors and an orange wash on the base of the tail. Both sexes have a dark stripe along the rear of the thigh.

Similar species: The dunes sagebrush lizard is of very restricted distribution and has a dark shoulder spot.

Taxonomic comments: The former subspecies *S. u. garmani* (northern prairie lizard), *S. u. tedbrowni* (Mescalero prairie lizard), and the Mexican *S. u. speari* (Cabeza de Vaca prairie lizard, no photo), are synonymized herein.

106. Southern Plateau Lizard

Sceloporus cowlesi

Abundance/Range: This is a fairly common lizard. It is found only at White Sands, New Mexico.

Habitat: This is an inhabitant of shifting, yielding sands where dwarfed oaks and sparse grasses grow.

Size: This small prairie lizard is adult at a total length of only 5 inches. The tail is about 150% of the SVL. Hatchlings are a bit less than 2 inches in total length.

Identifying features: This pallid lizard is tan to sand white with an obscure pattern. Except for its paleness it is quite like the southern form of the prairie lizard in appearance.

Similar species: The dunes sagebrush lizard is also very pale. However, it has small, nonkeeled scales on the rear of its thighs and is found only around Monahans, Texas, and near Roswell, New Mexico.

Comments: This species was formerly known as *S. u. cowlesi*, the White Sands prairie lizard.

ADDITIONAL SUBSPECIES

As currently understood, none.

Southern plateau lizard

107. Northern Plateau Lizard

Sceloporus tristichus

Abundance/Range: This is a common lizard. It is found in New Mexico, Arizona, and northward into southwestern Wyoming. There is a disjunct population in the Santa Catalina Mountains of Arizona.

Habitat: This is a high-altitude plateau lizard. It utilizes rocks, escarpments, stumps, shrubs, and grasses as habitats.

Size: Typically, adults measure 5 or 6 inches in length. Males may occasionally attain 7 inches in total length. The tail is about 150% of the SVL. Hatchlings are about 1¾ inches in total length.

Identifying features: This species tends to be vaguely striped in the south but unstriped farther north. There are about 10 pairs of dark spots from the nape to the base of the tail. Both sexes have blue on the belly and throat, but that of the male is much more intense than

Northern plateau lizard (southern form)

Northern plateau lizard (red-lipped form)

that of the female. In some populations, breeding males develop orange or red on their lips.

Similar species: Prairie and plateau lizards can be of quite similar appearance. However, the plateau lizard *usually* has less well-defined striping. Rely on range to help with identifications.

Comments: *S. u. elongata* (northern plateau lizard) and *S. u. erythrocheilus* (red-lipped plateau lizard) are now synonymized herein.

ADDITIONAL SUBSPECIES

As currently understood, none.

Northern plateau lizard (northern form)

108. Striped Plateau Lizard

Sceloporus virgatus

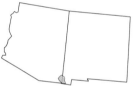

Abundance/Range: In the United States this abundant lizard is found only within a small range in extreme southwestern New Mexico and adjacent Arizona. It occurs also in northern Mexico.

Habitat: This is a species of rocky, open oak, oak-pine, and pine woodland, of rocky clearings, and rocky stream-edge situations. It prefers habitats between 5,000 and 10,000 feet in elevation.

Size: Large adults may attain 6⅞ inches in overall length, but are usually an inch or so smaller. The tail is about 150% of the SVL. Hatchlings are about 2¼ inches long.

Identifying features: Except for the grayish vertebral area, between the 2 very prominent yellowish dorsolateral stripes the back is reddish brown. A series of about 10 pairs of small darker markings nestles against the dorsolateral stripes. The dark markings may have a light inner edging. Between the dorsolateral stripes and the lateral stripes the upper sides are usually a bit darker than the back. The belly is light gray. There are no blue belly patches. Males have pale blue throat patches.

Striped plateau lizard

Similar species: This is the most prominently striped spiny lizard within its range. This should be diagnostic.

ADDITIONAL SUBSPECIES

None.

Fringe-toed Lizards, Genus *Uma*

This is a group of four described, and at least one yet-to-be-described specialized dwellers of desert dunes. These lizards require loose-sand habitat, a medium into which some (most?) startled fringe-toes dive nose-first and wriggle almost instantaneously from view. In our experience, the Yuman Desert fringe-toed lizard is more apt to dart into a rodent burrow than to dive into the sand.

109–113. Fringe-toed Lizards

Abundance/Range: These four species vary from common to uncommon. They occur on the Colorado, Mojave, and Yuma deserts.
Habitat: In order to exist, these lizards must have expanses of live dunes.
Size: These may attain an adult length of nearly 8 inches. Most are smaller.

Fringe-toed lizard rear foot

The tail length is about equal to the SVL. Hatchlings are about 2¾ inches in length.

Identifying features: All are robust but flattened, almost squat lizards, with a short tail and comblike fringes of scales along the outer edges of the rear toes. The fringes appear to be an adaptation to facilitate fast moves and faster turns on a substrate more yielding than most. The lower jaw is countersunk, the eyes have large, functional, overlapping lids, and the ears have fringe-edged flaps to help keep sand away from the tympanum. The nostrils are valvular and can be closed to prevent the entrance of sand granules. A lateral fold and a gular fold are present.

The shape and intensity of dark markings on the throat should aid with species identification.

Gravid females develop orange patches on their lower sides. One or more clutches of up to 6 eggs are laid annually. Reproductively active males develop a tinge of pink or pale green on the lower sides. There are 5–12 black markings on the underside of the tail, proximally in the form of spots, but widening to bars distally.

Similar species: None.

109. The Coachella Valley Fringe-toed Lizard, *Uma inornata*, is limited in distribution to the California Valley of that name (near the Salton Sea). Although still common in some dunes, much of its habitat has been altered by industry and agriculture. It is now an endangered species. This is a ghostly pale fringe-toe with a pattern of profuse dark-centered, chalk-white ocelli on the back and sides. The converging chin stripes are pale and often obscure. It lacks the pair of dark ventral spots present on all other species or, if the spots are present, they are greatly reduced in size or fragmented.

Coachella Valley fringe-toed lizard

Coachella Valley fringe-toed lizard, belly, no blotches

110. The Colorado Desert Fringe-toed Lizard, *Uma notata*, remains common on and near the Algodones and the Imperial Dunes of southeastern California. It is found west of the Colorado River. It also occurs on smaller dune systems. This pretty fringe-toe has buff-colored dorsal and lateral ocelli. The dark converging lines on the chin and the pair of black ventral spots are prominent.

Colorado Desert fringe-toed lizard

Colorado Desert fringe-toed lizard, belly, with blotches

111. The Yuman Desert Fringe-toed Lizard, *Uma rufopunctata*, is identical to the Colorado Desert fringe-toed lizard in appearance but differs genetically. It occurs east of the Colorado River in dunes in the Yuma Desert.

Yuman Desert Fringe-toed Lizard
Uma rufopunctata

Mohawk Dunes Fringe-toed Lizard
Uma species Cf rufopunctata

Yuman Desert fringe-toed lizard. Photo by Randy Babb

Mohawk Dunes fringe-toed lizard

112. Also similar in appearance to both the Colorado Desert and the Yuman Desert fringe-toed lizards, the population of fringe-toed lizards on the Mohawk Dunes of Arizona is supposedly distinct enough genetically to warrant its own taxonomy. It has not yet (August 2008) been described.

113. The Mojave Fringe-toed Lizard, *Uma scoparia*, is another richly colored *Uma*. The deep buff ocelli have reddish central spots. The pair of black belly spots is prominent. The dark lines on the chin form crescents rather than converging lines. This species ranges northwestward from Bouse, Arizona to the vicinity of Death Valley, California.

Mojave fringe-toed lizard

Tree Lizards and Brush Lizards, Genus *Urosaurus*

The tree lizards are a group of six confusingly similar and possibly invalid subspecies. They are slender, long limbed, and long tailed. A gular fold and a lateral fold are present.

Subspecies are differentiated largely by the arrangement and comparative size of the vertebral and paravertebral scale rows. It will be necessary to have this lizard in hand to determine the comparative sizes of these scales.

Brush lizards are more elongate and often of more pallid coloration.

The lizards of this genus are oviparous and fecund. Large healthy females may lay up to 6 clutches containing 6–16 eggs each. Although not particularly spooky, once alerted, these lizards may be difficult to approach closely.

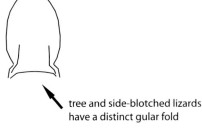

tree and side-blotched lizards have a distinct gular fold

Move slowly and obliquely (rather than straight toward the lizard). Attempt not to make eye contact. These lizards frequent trees, shrubs, rocks, and escarpments in desert canyons. The digits bear sharp claws but are not expanded into pads.

114. Western Long-tailed Brush Lizard

Urosaurus graciosus graciosus

Abundance/Range: This lizard ranges southward from southern Nevada to Northern Baja and from eastern California to western Arizona. It can be quite common in some regions but blends so well with the leafless branches of the shrubs where it is found that it is often overlooked.

Habitat: This is an aridland and semi-aridland species found on creosote flats as well as in association with mesquite and thornscrub.

Size: The overall length is about 7½ inches. The tail is 190%–210% of the SVL. Hatchlings are about 3 inches long.

Identifying features: This is a slender lizard that is usually of pallid coloration. The ground color blends well with the dried, slender limbs on which it often positions itself lengthwise. There are dark bars on the back and on the surface of the tail. If the lizard is undisturbed the dark bars may contrast sharply with the dorsal color, but they quickly become imperceptible if the lizard is frightened. There is a band of enlarged scales along the middle of the back. Males have a bluish

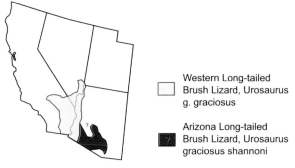

Western Long-tailed Brush Lizard, Urosaurus g. graciosus

Arizona Long-tailed Brush Lizard, Urosaurus graciosus shannoni

Western long-tailed brush lizard

green patch on each side of the belly, and both males and females may have an orange or yellow throat.

Similar species: Other brush and tree lizards have a proportionately shorter tail and a more contrasting dorsal pattern.

ADDITIONAL SUBSPECIES

115. The Arizona Long-tailed Brush Lizard, *Urosaurus graciosus shannoni,* is of questionable subspecific validity. It supposedly differs from the western form only in having a more contrasting pattern and brilliant colors. It is found from southwestern Arizona to central Arizona.

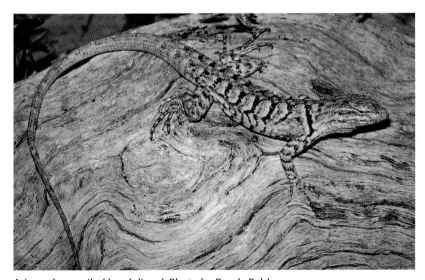

Arizona long-tailed brush lizard. Photo by Randy Babb

116. Baja California Brush Lizard

Urosaurus nigricaudus

Abundance/Range: This lizard ranges southward from southwestern California to the southern tip of the Baja Peninsula. It is a common species.

Habitat: This species may be found across a broad spectrum of habitats. It can be seen on fallen trees, stumps, rocks, escarpments, construction rubble, and buildings.

Size: This lizard attains 5 inches in total length. The tail is 150%–175% of the SVL. Hatchlings are about 2¼ inches long.

Identifying features: The coloration is variable but is usually of some shade of tan to dull russet. Six to 8 dark crossbands, often broken medially by a gray stripe, are on the back. The first crossband may appear collarlike. The sides are often more richly colored than the back. A band of enlarged scales runs from shoulder to tail base. Males have blue patches on the belly and a orangish yellow throat. Females have a yellow throat but no blue on the belly. The tail is dark, often black distally. These lizards may be light colored at one moment and a good deal darker just a minute or two later.

Similar species: In some of its phases, the ornate tree lizard can be difficult to differentiate. See account 117.

Baja California brush lizard

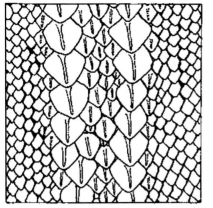
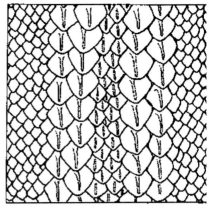

Size and arrangement of dorsal scales may help to identify tree lizard subspecies

Tree lizard dorsal scales, diagrammatic, by Kenneth P. Wray III

ADDITIONAL SUBSPECIES

None.

117. Ornate Tree Lizard

Urosaurus ornatus ssp.

Abundance/Range: These are abundant but easily overlooked lizards. The range of the combined subspecies includes extreme southern Wyoming, then southward to northern Mexico.

Habitat: Despite their common name, tree lizards are entirely at home on canyon faces, escarpments, and boulders, as well as on trees.

Size: This slender, somewhat flattened lizard attains a maximum length of about 5¼ inches. The tail is about 160% of the SVL. Hatchlings are about 1½ inches in overall length.

Identifying features: The subtle dorsal hues and patterns blend almost imperceptibly into the rocks and bark on which these lizards live.

The dorsal ground color can be gray to brown. The back is marked with about 6 pairs of darker spots or bars. The markings may be highlighted by light tan or by rust or blue. The belly of the

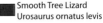
Smooth Tree Lizard
Urosaurus ornatus levis

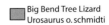
Big Bend Tree Lizard
Urosaurus o. schmidti

Schott's Tree Lizard
Urosaurus o. schottii

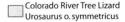
Colorado River Tree Lizard
Urosaurus o. symmetricus

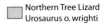
Northern Tree Lizard
Urosaurus o. wrighti

female is grayish, her throat is yellowish. Two large turquoise ventrolateral markings replace most of the gray on the belly of the male. The throat is yellowish but often has a turquoise central area. A prominent gular fold exists and a fold of loose skin is apparent along each side. The tail is prominently barred, the limbs more obscurely so.

Similar species: Other species in this genus lack the small scales that separate the paravertebral rows of large scales.

Comments: Many researchers feel that there are no populations of tree lizard distinct enough to be afforded subspecific status. Certainly the intrapopulational characteristics of most are variable and many criteria currently used for subspecific differentiation are broadly overlapping. We have listed the occasionally assigned subspecific names below.

ADDITIONAL SUBSPECIES

117a. The Smooth Tree Lizard, *Urosaurus ornatus levis*, is found in central northern New Mexico. It usually has 4 rows of enlarged scales along the back that are not separated vertebrally by a row of smaller scales. The belly patches usually do not touch.

117b. The Big Bend Tree Lizard, *Urosaurus ornatus schmidti*, occurs only in Texas' Big Bend and Trans-Pecos regions and immediately adjacent New Mexico and Mexico. The paravertebral rows of enlarged scales are

Smooth tree lizard

Big Bend tree lizard

less than twice as large as the smaller outermost rows. The belly patches are usually widely separated.

117c. Schott's Tree Lizard, *Urosaurus ornatus schottii*, now contains the subspecies formerly known as *U. o. linearis*. It ranges through most of Arizona, western New Mexico, and from there well into Mexico. The 2 bands of enlarged scales are separated by 2 or 3 rows of small vertebral scales. The belly patches are narrowly separated or may touch medially.

Schott's tree lizard

Schott's tree lizard, belly

117d. The Colorado River Tree Lizard, *Urosaurus ornatus symmetricus*, ranges northward from northeastern Baja California and southeastern California to southeastern Nevada and western Arizona. The two bands of enlarged paravertebral scales are separated by several rows of small scales that are, together, wider than the width of the band of large scales. The belly patches are usually widely separated.

Colorado River tree lizard

Northern tree lizard

117e. The Northern Tree Lizard, *Urosaurus ornatus wrighti*, is found from south central Wyoming to northern Arizona and northern New Mexico. The band of enlarged scales is 3 or 4 scales wide and not separated vertebrally. The belly patches usually touch.

Side-blotched Lizards, Genus *Uta*

Despite being alert, these small desert iguanians will allow close approach by a slow-moving observer. When frightened, side-blotched lizards will dart to the safety of a grass clump, to the far side of or beneath a rock, or possibly into a convenient small mammal burrow. This is one of the most commonly encountered lizards in the American west.

The black spot behind the forelimb and lack of rose-colored belly blotches are diagnostic.

Several clutches of 1–4 (rarely to 6) eggs are produced annually.

118. Side-blotched Lizard

Uta stansburiana ssp.

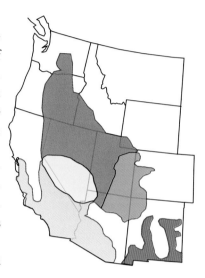

Abundance/Range: This group of five subspecies is among the most abundant of lizards throughout their combined ranges. Collectively they range southward from central Washington to the southern tip of the Baja Peninsula and from northern Texas to northern Mexico.

Habitat: These are terrestrial and rock-dwelling species. They may be seen basking on low natural and manmade prominences: rocks, abutments, and dirt-clods among them.

Size: Although adult at 3½–4½ inches in total length, occasional specimens may attain 5¼ inches. Males are the larger sex. The tail is about 175% of the SVL. Despite the rather small size of the adults, hatchlings may measure a comparatively large 2½ inches.

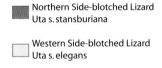

Northern Side-blotched Lizard
Uta s. stansburiana

Western Side-blotched Lizard
Uta s. elegans

Nevada Side-blotched Lizard
Uta s. nevadensis

Eastern Side-blotched Lizard
Uta s. stejnegeri

Plateau Side-blotched Lizard
Uta s. uniformis

Identifying features: The dorsal colors of this species blend well with the soils on which the lizard lives. The ground color may be tan, fawn, olive brown, reddish, or almost white. Females have prominent, thin, light dorsolateral lines, and rather regularly arranged, pale dorsal and lateral spots. Males have a pale or nonexistent dorsolateral line and a dorsum heavily flecked with lighter (interspersed with bright blue) spots. The sides may be brighter than the back. The male's tail may be bluish. Dorsal and lateral scales are small and weakly keeled, giving a sandpapery texture to the upper surfaces. A prominent gular fold is present. Hatchlings have very prominent dorsolateral stripes. Males may have a bluish venter and a dusky chin with a blue center. Females have a light chin and venter.

Similar species: Most spiny lizards have heavily keeled, spiny scales and are larger. Tree lizards lack the black spot posterior to the arm.

Comments: The field marks used to identify the subspecies of this lizard overlap broadly or may be apparent on only one sex. Many researchers question the validity of the subspecies. Although we have listed them below we also urge that you use range as an identification tool.

ADDITIONAL SUBSPECIES

118a. The Northern Side-blotched Lizard, *Uta stansburiana stansburiana*, has weakly keeled dorsal scales. The dorsolateral stripes of females may be broken or lacking. Males have a profusion of blue dorsal spots. This subspecies ranges northward from eastern California and northwestern Arizona to central Nevada and western Utah.

Northern side-blotched lizard

118b. The Western Side-blotched Lizard, *Uta stansburiana elegans*, has prominent dorsolateral stripes and blue dorsal spots, and ranges southward from southern California and western Arizona to southern Sonora, Mexico.

118c. The Nevada Side-blotched Lizard, *Uta stansburiana nevadensis*, is weakly marked dorsally. Breeding males develop orange sides. Actually, this is the northernmost subspecies, occurring from northern Nevada to central Washington and southeastern Idaho.

Western side-blotched lizard

Nevada side-blotched lizard. Photo by R. W. Van Devender

118d. The Eastern Side-blotched Lizard, *Uta stansburiana stejnegeri*, is a colorful form and the only one of the five subspecies having a disjunct range. The dorsolateral stripes are best defined anteriorly. Breeding males are spangled with turquoise dorsal spots and have a blue tail. This form ranges southward from central New Mexico and northern Texas to central Mexico.

Eastern side-blotched lizard

118e. The Plateau Side-blotched Lizard, *Uta stansburiana uniformis*, is weakly marked and often orangish in color. It occurs in the high country of the Four Corners region.

Plateau side-blotched lizard

ANOLES, FAMILY POLYCHROTIDAE

Only three species of anoles, the green (native), the brown (introduced), and the knight (also introduced), occur in our coverage area. Males are territorial and aggressive, especially during the spring and summer breeding season. Territorial and breeding displays are species specific. These displays include dewlap distension, lateral body flattening, push-ups, temporary erection of glandular nape and vertebral crests, and intimidating sidles.

Dewlap coloration is often species-diagnostic for human observers. It is, apparently, even more so for the lizards themselves that perceive and respond to ultraviolet reflections from the dewlaps.

Anoles are oviparous. Reproduction is stimulated by the progressively increasing daylengths of spring and terminates in late summer. After an initial annual breeding, sperm retention results in fertile eggs when the female is stimulated solely by courtship displays. One or two eggs may be laid at two week or somewhat longer intervals. Anoles often prepare no actual nest, instead nudging their eggs into the protection of a grass clump, into a bromeliad leaf axil, or between fallen leaves with their snout. Incubation may vary between 35 and 65 days.

The green anole is capable of undergoing dramatic color changes. The brown anole merely changes shades of brown. Color changes are in response to temperature and stress level rather than to background, although remarkable camouflage may result.

Distended, elongate (teardrop-shaped) toepads are characteristic.

American Color-changers

An-oles they're usually called. And it is by that pronunciation that almost everyone knows the lizards. But if you wish to be absolutely correct, call then an-ole-ees.

Of the U.S. states, Florida has had the dubious distinction of being anole central. Not only is the green anole native to Florida, but about ten other species from the West Indies and Latin America have become tenuously to firmly entrenched in the state. The most successful of these species has been the little Cuban brown anoles, which first overran Florida from the south northward and then spread beyond the state into southeastern Georgia and some areas of Texas. These were followed by the immense knight anoles and several other species.

Now three species of these lacertilian colonists, the green anole, *Anolis carolinensis*, the brown anole, *A. sagrei*, and the western knight anole, *A. equestris*, have in some way made their way to and become established on the islands of Hawaii. Two species, the brown and the knight anole, seem still restricted to Oahu, but the green anole occurs on all of the main islands.

The anoles are climbers par excellence. They have not only sharp claws, but also expanded, elongate, digital pads that allow them to easily traverse smooth vertical surfaces. Many of the canopy species (such as the green and the knight anoles) readily and rapidly change color from bright green to the deepest of browns. Tree-bole species, such as the brown anole, change only the hues of brown in which they are clad. Males of all, and both sexes of some, have a distensible throat dewlap that is used during territorial displays and courtship. The dewlap varies in color by species, and because of ultraviolet reflections is apparently perceived differently by the lizards than by humans.

The brown and the green anoles are adult at about 8 inches in total length. The knight anole is the largest species in the genus and nears 20 inches in length. The females of all are smaller than the males.

Look for all in and on ornamental and native shade trees, palms, and large shrubs.

119. Green Anole

Anolis carolinensis carolinensis

Abundance/Range: This pretty lizard has been known to be an established resident on the Hawaiian chain since prior to 1950. It is widespread on Hawaii, Oahu, and Maui and is more locally distributed on the other main islands. It has recently been found in the vicinity of Los Angeles, California, but its pop-

Green anole

ulation statistics in that area are not known. It also occurs along the Gulf Coast and in the southeastern United States, where it is native.

Habitat: This species is strongly arboreal. It favors tall grasses, shrubs, and trees. It may be abundant in ecotones where one type of habitat abuts another. It often hangs head-down on trunks, wooden fence posts, and other such vantage points.

Size: Large males may attain a total length of 8 inches. The tail is nearly twice as long as the SVL. Females are noticeably the smaller sex. Hatchlings are a bit more than 2 inches long.

Identifying features: Because green anoles have the ability to change color, they are often (and erroneously) referred to as chameleons. Resting and content anoles tend to be of some shade of brown, but may be bright green. They are darker when cold, and turn a pasty gray when overly warm. Disturbed anoles may be patchy brown and green. Males involved in aggression are often bright green with a nearly black ear-patch. Breeding males are often green but lack the dark ear-patch. Female green anoles have a light vertebral line. Displaying males can erect a low vertebral crest on the nape and anterior trunk. Throughout most of the green anole's range, males have a decidedly red to pink dewlap. If a dewlap is present on a female, it is vestigial.

Similar species: Within the scope of this guide, only this species, the huge knight anole, and yellow-crested Jackson's chameleon have the ability to change body color from green to brown. The knight anole has yellow flash marks below the eye and on the shoulder. The chameleon is laterally flattened and has a strongly serrate crest, and males have 3 prominent facial horns.

Comments: These are shy lizards that will sidle to the far side of a tree trunk or post or dart upward into the canopy if approached by day. They are more easily approached at night, when they sleep soundly resting on grasses or the upper side of flat leaves.

120. Western Knight Anole

Anolis equestris equestris

Abundance/Range: This is a common but not always easily found anole. It is locally distributed and known only from Oahu in the Hawaiian chain. It also occurs in Broward, Collier, Martin, Monroe, Palm Beach, and St. Lucie counties, Florida. The knight anole is of Cuban origin.

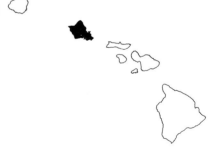

Habitat: Knight anoles are primarily, but not exclusively, canopy denizens. When the weather is very warm, knight anoles descend more frequently from the canopy and station themselves in a head down position, low on the trunks of palms and other ornamental trees. This lizard is very conspicuous when a very territorial male fans its immense pink dewlap.

Size: This is the largest of all known anoles. Male knight anoles occasionally exceed a total length of 18 inches. The tail is about 150% of the SVL. Females are somewhat smaller. Hatchlings are about 3 inches long.

Western knight anole

Identifying features: Like many other canopy anoles, the knight anole has the ability to change color dramatically. When warm and unstressed, it is usually bright green with yellow flash marks below each eye and on each shoulder. If cold or frightened, the lizard quickly darkens its color to chocolate brown or almost black. The flash markings remain visible. Yellow bands may show on the tail, and light (cream to yellow) interstitial (between scales) skin may be visible. Through muscle contractions, the knight anole can raise a low vertebral crest and a much more prominent nuchal crest. The head is large and bony. Both sexes have dewlaps and indulge in territorial displays.

Similar species: No other U.S. anole has as large and bony a head, nor do any attain as great a size as adult knight anoles. The yellow to white flash marks are diagnostic.

Comments: The knight anole will bite painfully if carelessly restrained. When threatened by a predator (including humans) or when involved in territorial displays, the lizard generally gapes widely, distends its dewlap, and turns its laterally flattened body sideways to the threat.

121. Brown Anole

Anolis sagrei

Abundance/Range: This lizard was origi-nally introduced on Oahu, Hawaii, prior to 1980. Since it readily colonizes tropical regions, it is a bit surprising that it has not yet been found on other islands in the Hawaiian chain. Elsewhere, this species occurs in Texas, Florida, Cuba, the Bahamas, and at various points in Latin America.

Habitat: This is a lizard that thrives in disturbed habitats and among ornamental plantings. Although often seen low in trees and shrubs, this lizard is quite terrestrial. If frightened, it often darts to cover on the ground.

Size: Males attain a total length of about 8 inches. Females are substantially smaller. Hatchlings are about 2 inches long.

Identifying features: The brown anole is aptly named. Both males and females are of some shade of brown. The males often have bands of light (yellowish) spots and are darkest dorsally. Males can erect a nuchal, vertebral, and anterior caudal ridge. This is best developed on the nape and anterior trunk. The dewlap of the brown anole may vary from quite a bright red orange to a rather pale yellow. The edge of the dewlap is white. When the dewlap is not distended, the white edging is visible as a white stripe on the throat. Female and juvenile brown anoles have a dark, scal-

Brown anole, adult male

loped-edged, light vertebral stripe. The belly is brown on the sides and gray centrally.

Similar species: When in its brown phase, the green anole is slimmer and males have a red to pink dewlap that lacks a white edging. Only the brown anole has a white stripe on the throat when the dewlap is not distended.

Comments: These are feisty anoles that bluff and display throughout each of the warm days of the year. They are somewhat less aggressive (but far from benign) during the nonreproductive winter days. Brown anoles will even distend their dewlaps and indulge in agonistic behavior if a human makes eye contact and bobs his/her head at the lizard.

Brown anole, adult female

Brown anole, aberrant adult male

16

Old World Wall Lizards

Family Lacertidae

This large family, commonly referred to as lacertids, consists of very typical-appearing lizards of Old World origin. Within the family are a few large and a great many many small species. The largest is the eyed lizard, *Timon* (*Lacerta*) *lepida*, a beautiful species that can occasionally exceed 2 feet in length. Lacertids can autotomize and regenerate the tail, but the regrown appendage is quite different in appearance than the original.

In habits and general appearance the lacertids look much like our racerunners and whiptails (family Teiidae). The lizards of both families are nervous, wary, and quick to react to what they consider adverse stimuli (such as the approach of a human). When foraging, the members of both families move in short spurts of motion, probing with their nose into all manner of nooks and crannies, and scratching insect prey from beneath the sand-surface with quick motions of the forelimbs. Fruit and blossoms are also eaten.

The lacertids are sun worshippers, usually not emerging from their lairs until the ground is well warmed. When basking, many species flatten their bodies and angle toward the sun to more quickly warm themselves.

This family is represented in the west by a single species of introduced wall lizard of the genus *Podarcis*.

This oviparous lizard lays 3–6 eggs in a clutch, and more than a single clutch may be produced annually by a healthy female.

OLD WORLD WALL LIZARDS, GENUS *PODARCIS*

These are small, active Old World lizards. The single species to occur in western North America is apparently rather well established on southern Vancouver Island, British Columbia. The lizards of this genus have 6 rows of plates on the belly. These lizards often allow rather close approach before darting to safety, but are adept at evading capture.

122. Common Wall Lizard

Podarcis muralis

Abundance/Range: Populations of this lizard are known to have existed in the vicinity of Victoria, Vancouver Island, British Columbia, since the early 1970s. It is a native of much of Europe.

Habitat: This little lizard of urban areas is particularly abundant in areas where construction rubble has accumulated, near old houses, along stone and brick walls, where sidewalks are broken and slightly tipped, and in gardens.

Size: One of the smaller lacertids, the common wall lizard is adult at 6–8 inches. Its long tail is 200% of SVL. Hatchlings are about 2½ inches long.

Common wall lizard

Identifying features: This is a small, slender lizard that flattens itself noticeably when basking. Both color and pattern are variable, but the back is usually predominantly tan to fawn with or without darker markings. The sides are nearly black and bear round to oval gray blue spots. The sides of the lower jaw and jowls may be grayish blue. Females are usually the more colorful sex. The 6 rows of rectangular belly scales may be white to orange red.

Similar species: None. Although this little lizard looks much like a small whiptail, no whiptails occur in Canada. The rounded lateral spots will identify this species.

17

Skinks

Family Scincidae

This large family contains more than 1,200 species that vary from small to large in size and from secretive to overtly apparent in habits. The lizards of the family occur on all continents except Antarctica. Skinks are often present on islands, keys, and atolls. Some of the largest species occur on the Solomon Islands, Australia, and New Guinea. Species may inhabit rain forest or desert as well as most habitats in between these two extremes. Skinks may be arboreal, terrestrial, fossorial, or semiaquatic. They may lay eggs or produce live young. In both modes of reproduction, the maximum clutch size appears to be about 24. The Solomon Island giant skink routinely has only one (rarely two) large, live babies.

Many species of skink undergo remarkable ontogenetic changes. The hatchlings of some are vividly striped with yellow against a black ground color and may have a vivid blue, pink, or red tail. These colors usually fade with growth, and the adults are a uniform brown or tan. Sexual dimorphism may or may not be marked. Males of many species develop a fiery orange head and enlarged temporal area when they are reproductively active.

Many species are insectivorous, but some specialize in a diet of worms. A few eat crabs, other lizards, or even nestling rodents. Many larger species are herbivorous or omnivorous.

Skinks have shiny cycloid scales that overlay bony osteoderms. The scales of most species are smooth, but some may have weakly keeled, strongly keeled, or even spiny scales.

Among the lizards of this family, many are burrowing species with limbs that are reduced in size, sometimes in number, or entirely absent. When legs are present, toes may be reduced in number. Burrowing species may also have eyes so reduced in size that they are nonfunctional, and the ear openings of some are covered with scales.

A few species are so specialized that they are able to literally swim through the desert sands.

The several prehensile-tailed species of the New Guinea genus *Praeso-haema* have green blood.

Skinks often make a very audible rustling when darting away from danger. Most will bite if carelessly restrained; the bite of the large species can be painful.

Taxonomic note: The skinks of western continental United States are all in the genus *Plestiodon* (formerly *Eumeces*), but the introduced Hawaiian species are contained in four additional genera, *Cryptoblepharus*, *Emoia*, *Lampropholis*, and *Lipinia*.

Skinks: The Bluest of Blues

There are blues, and then there are blues, and many shades of this wonderful color occur on the tails of the various skinks. There is the deep azure shade of the tail of the juvenile Great Plains skink, and the light soft blue seen on juvenile variable skinks. And, once seen, the intensity of color on the tail of juvenile Skilton's skinks is certainly memorable. But light or dark, bright or dull, in my opinion, no other blue on a skink's tail can equal that of the mountain skink, *Plestiodon callicephalus*, in sheer beauty. It is the bluest of blues, the purest of pures, and the brightest of brights!

I had been wanting to see a mountain skink for some time, so when Randy Babb said, "Let's go find one," we went to find one.

We hopped on the interstate and sped south out of Phoenix. Then right, left, and park. Then we walked—and we walked and we walked and we walked: through desert, around a lake, through more desert, over boulders. Randy was like a mountain goat. I struggled to keep pace—or at least not to lose sight of him. Finally we were at the bed of a stream, long dry in appearance, but just awaiting a desert rainstorm to become active again. Oh, and did I mention that it was hot? And dry? And *very* hot?

Eventually Randy stopped and began flipping rocks. "Here's one!" he suddenly exclaimed, then added, "But it got away."

continued

This wasn't surprising, for ten million rocks abutted and topped one another, and unless the skink was particularly slow or very understanding, it would take an immediate knuckle-skinning grab to catch it.

"Here's another! Darn. It got away too. Whoops. Another. Got it!" And so it was 1 for 3 for Randy. Zero for zero for me. I hadn't even seen one. But it mattered not, for the mountain skink caught by Randy epitomized everything I had ever come to believe about the lizard. The warm brown body bore light-edged dark lateral stripes and a pattern of light stripes on the top of its head. But it was the tail that stopped me in my tracks. It was a beautiful electric robin's egg blue! How could such a marvelous color have developed on such a secretive lizard? And why?

SNAKE-EYED SKINKS, GENUS *CRYPTOBLEPHARUS*

A genus of small arboreal and rock-dwelling skinks, the snake-eyed skinks occur on Madagascar, Australia, and other regions in Oceania. The members of this genus have fused, immovable eyelids. The lower eyelid contains a transparent spectacle that allows the lizard to see well. The single Hawaiian species is thought to have been present on these islands prior to the arrival of Europeans.

123. Snake-eyed Skink

Cryptoblepharus poecilopleurus

Abundance/Range: This skink is found on all the main Hawaiian Islands as well as some smaller islands. The snake-eyed skink has seemingly become rare in Hawaii, but it is secretive and easily overlooked. It is locally distributed.

Habitat: Although it is occasionally found in inland habitats, on the Hawaiian Islands this skink is most often associated with rocky coastal habitats. It may occur in seawalls, rock walls along boundary lines, and jumbles of boulders, on open rocky beaches, or near trees and shrubs growing along the beach.

Snake-eyed skink. Photo by Gerald McCormack

Size: The snake-eyed skink is adult at 4–5 inches in total length. The tail is about 150% of SVL. Hatchlings of this oviparous species are about 2 inches in total length.

Identifying features: This is a small, slender skink. The back is fawn to gray either with or without lighter mottling. The sides and limbs are darker gray or black with light mottling. Most exhibit a pair of poorly defined yellowish lines running from the rear of the head, along the upper sides, onto the tail. The upper surface of the tail is light tan or gray with a dark central stripe for about half its length. The belly is off-white to pale yellow. This skink has immovable eyelids.

Similar species: All other skinks on the Hawaiian Islands have functional (movable) eyelids.

ADDITIONAL SUBSPECIES

None.

EMOIAS, GENUS *EMOIA*

This is a large genus of terrestrial and arboreal skinks that are distributed throughout Oceania. Although the eyelids are functional, the lower lid contains a transparent spectacle, allowing vision when the eye is closed. The emoias are oviparous and of moderate size. Two species were historically known to inhabit Hawaii, but one, the Azure-tailed skink, *Emoia impar*, seems no longer present in Hawaii. Although referred to as the azure-tailed skink, the tail may actually be brown or greenish in color. Equally variable, the ground color may be brown or black and stripes may be present or absent. Reptiles occasionally reappear after having seemed extirpated for long periods, so we have provided a photograph of the striped phase of the azure-tailed skink.

Azure-tailed skink. Photo by Gerald McCormack

124. Copper-tailed Skink

Emoia cyanura

Abundance/Range: This is a rare species in Hawaii; it is restricted to only a few areas on Kauai. It is more common on many islands elsewhere in Oceania.

Habitat: This skink may be found on rocks, amid ground litter, in grasslands, and at woodland edge. It is often seen near fallen logs and in woodpiles. Although predominantly terrestrial, it can climb well.

Size: This long-tailed skink reaches an adult overall size of about 6 inches. Most are somewhat smaller. The tail is about 150% of SVL. Hatchlings are about 2 inches in total length.

Identifying features: This is a rather slender skink with a narrow head and pointed snout. The ground color is brown to olive brown dorsally. The sides and belly are light. There are usually 3 prominent yellowish stripes on the top of the head and the back, but occasionally the dorsolateral pair are faded and indistinct. In Hawaii, the tail is copper, orange, or greenish. Interestingly, on other islands this skink may have a bright blue tail and is then referred to as the "azure-tailed skink."

Copper-tailed skink. Photo by Gerald McCormack

Similar species: No other Hawaiian skink has 3 prominent yellowish stripes on the back.

ADDITIONAL SUBSPECIES

None in Hawaii.

METALLIC SKINKS, GENUS *LAMPROPHOLIS*

This is another large skink genus of the Oceania geographic region. All members of the genus are oviparous, and all are small, slender, and have well-developed legs. Most species have 5 toes on each foot; at least one (an Australian species) has only 4 toes on each of the forefeet. The eyelids are functional; the lower lid has a transparent window. These are small, slender, terrestrial skinks that prefer well-lit, moist, or frequently watered habitats.

125. Metallic Skink

Lampropholis delicata

Abundance/Range: This is the most abundant of the Hawaiian skinks. A very efficient insectivore, it is often speculated that this species contributes to population reductions in other Hawaiian skink species. The metallic skink is found on all of the major and some of the smaller Hawaiian Islands as well as on Australia and other islands.

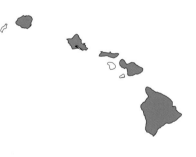

Habitat: Another of the terrestrial skink species, this secretive lizard may be found in most suitable habitats. Expect to see it in areas of leaf litter, rocks, and irrigated gardens. It may be common near tree buttresses and at treefalls.

Size: Because it is so slender this skink seems smaller than it actually is. Adult are between 3½ and 5 inches in total length. The long tail is about 150% of SVL. Hatchlings are about 1¾ inches long.

Identifying features: This shiny skink has a brown back, darker upper sides, and a light belly. The dark sides are bordered above by a thin darker

Metallic skink. Photo by R. W. Van Devender

or lighter line and below by a gray to yellow line. The thin bordering lines may be difficult to see. The tail is grayish (sometimes with a vague bluish overcast) to brown. Breeding males develop a rusty hue on the otherwise brown head.

Similar species: The snake-eyed skink is mottled on both back and sides and does not have functional eyelids. The moth skink has a yellow blotch on the rear of its head.

ADDITIONAL SUBSPECIES

None.

MOTH SKINKS, GENUS *LIPINIA*

The more than 20 species in this genus are widely distributed in Oceania. They are generally associated with natural and artificial ground surface cover, but they may also burrow into loose substrates or seek shelter behind bark shards on standing and fallen trees. These small skinks are insectivorous and, temperatures permitting, may be active from dawn until late dusk.

This is another of the skinks thought to have been present on the Hawaiian Islands prior to the arrival of Europeans.

Eyelids are functional.

126. Moth Skink

Lipinia noctua noctua

Abundance/Range: This skink is moderately rare on all of the main Hawaiian Islands. It is common to abundant elsewhere in Oceania.

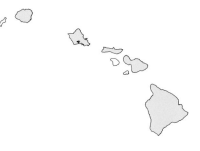

Habitat: Look for this tiny lizard amid leaf litter, beneath logs and rocks, and in tree buttresses along streambeds, as well as in lushly planted suburban and urban yards.

Size: The total length of this slender lizard is about 4 inches. Of this, slightly more than half is tail length, equal to about 120% of SVL. Neonates of this live-bearing skink are about 2 inches in length at birth.

Identifying features: Were it not for the yellow cranial spot and faded vertebral stripe, this would be a nondescript lizard. The sides are dark brown. The back is lighter brown, usually with small darker spots along each side of the vertebral stripe. The tail is light brown above. The belly is brown, and the underside of the tail is gray. The upper and lower labial (lip) scales bear short, vertical, light gray bars. Females give birth to small numbers of live young, often only 2.

Similar species: No other lizard species in Hawaii has the yellow spot on the top rear of the head.

Comments: The example depicted is from New Guinea. It is a bit more brightly colored than Hawaiian examples.

ADDITIONAL SUBSPECIES

None in Hawaii.

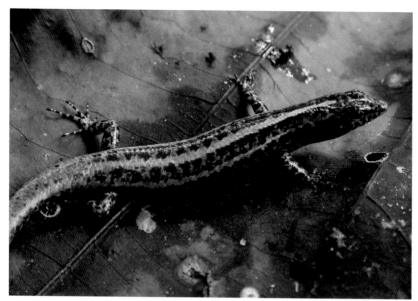

Moth skink. Photo by Fred Kraus

GREATER SKINKS, GENUS *PLESTIODON*

This is the predominant skink genus in the continental United States. It is more widely speciated in the eastern and central states than in the west, where only five species occur.

Western skinks tend to prefer rocky habitats that retain at least a vestige of moisture. When conditions are suitable the skinks may be found, sometimes in quite considerable numbers, beneath rocks, in rodent burrows, or along ponds, cattle tanks or other watercourses.

The greater skinks are very secretive, often thermoregulating by staying underneath and in contact with a sun-warmed rock. Considerable populations may exist but be unsuspected. These skinks are alert, fast moving, and difficult to approach.

Many species undergo dramatic age-related color and pattern changes. Juveniles are often prominently striped and have a brightly colored tail. These colors fade with growth. The adults are often a uniform brown, but may develop widened, fire orange heads when reproductively active. Males are often more brightly colored than the females.

All, except for one species, the mountain skink, are oviparous (and it sometimes lays eggs).

The 5–25 eggs are laid in moisture-retaining piles of ground debris, under fallen logs, in depressions beneath flat rocks, or in the burrows of small mammals. Larger females produce larger clutches of larger eggs. The female often remains in attendance of the clutch throughout the 45–65-day incubation period.

127. Mountain Skink

Plestiodon callicephalus

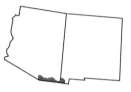

Abundance/Range: Although it has a wide range in Mexico, this skink barely enters the United States. It is very secretive and difficult to find, and population statistics are largely unknown. Within the range of this guide this skink occurs in extreme southeastern Arizona and immediately adjacent New Mexico.

Habitat: This skink seems most common near intermittent streams in rocky canyons of southeastern Arizona. It may be found from about sea level to 6,500 feet in elevation.

Mountain skink, subadult

Size: The total adult size of this skink is about 5 inches. The tail is a bit longer than the snout-vent length. Hatchlings/neonates are about 2 inches in length.

Identifying features: The adults of this 4-lined species are pretty. The babies are remarkably pretty. The back is a warm brown, the sides are darker. The dark color of the sides is bordered above and below by a yellowish line. The belly is light. A light Y is present on the top of the head. The tail of the adult is a dull but distinct blue. The tail of the juvenile is a robin's egg blue so intense it seems to glow.

Similar species: None. The 4 stripes and brilliant blue tail of the mountain skink are distinctive.

ADDITIONAL SUBSPECIES

None.

128. Gilbert's Skink
Plastiodon gilberti (species complex)

Taxonomic comments: This large skink is now thought to be a species complex rather than just a single variable form. Although morphological characters now used to identify the subspecies of *P. gilberti* are variable and overlapping, an actual reclassification has not yet been undertaken. For the moment we continue to recognize five races.

128a. Greater Brown Skink
Plestiodon gilberti gilberti

Abundance/Range: This large skink may be common to actually abundant in areas of suitable habitat. It is seen most frequently in the early spring and can be difficult to locate when habitats become dry. This is the subspecies of brown skink of the central Sierra Nevadas.

Habitat: This skink is a denizen of moist rock-strewn hillsides, stream edges, and rocky mountainside habitats. It burrows readily and also utilizes mammal burrows as the winds of spring and summer dry its habitat. This subspecies may range in altitude from the foothills to about 7,300 feet in elevation in the Sierras.

Size: This is the largest skink of the Pacific and southwestern states. Adult

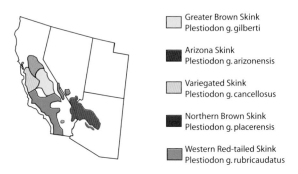

Greater Brown Skink
Plestiodon g. gilberti

Arizona Skink
Plestiodon g. arizonensis

Variegated Skink
Plestiodon g. cancellosus

Northern Brown Skink
Plestiodon g. placerensis

Western Red-tailed Skink
Plestiodon g. rubricaudatus

males of 10 inches in length are not uncommon, and the record size is 12¾ inches. Females are smaller. The tail of an adult is about 120% of the SVL; tails of younger individuals are proportionately longer.

Identifying features: This skink undergoes marked ontogenetic changes. The hatchlings are black with a series of vivid and well-defined straw yellow or tan stripes and with a bright blue tail. The scales within the light stripes usually have dark edges. With age the stripes fade until as adults the skinks have lost most of the striping. Except for the orange blush of their head, males become a uniform warm brown or olive brown. During the spring breeding season, the head widens posteriorly and becomes

Greater brown skink, adult non-breeding male

an intense fiery orange. Breeding females do not develop as bright a head color, nor does their head widen. Adult males in breeding color are spectacular.

Similar species: It may be very difficult to differentiate the Skilton's skink from the Gilbert's skink. See also accounts 132, 133, and 134.

ADDITIONAL SUBSPECIES

Because of the variability of morphological characters and a great deal of intergradation, the subspecies of the brown skink can be difficult to differentiate. It is the juveniles that vary the most. Use the range maps.

128b. Adult Arizona Brown Skinks, *Plestiodon g. arizonensis*, may retain some striping. The juveniles have a pink(ish) tail that is dullest above. This subspecies is of questionable validity. It ranges from central Arizona to southern Nevada.

Arizona brown skink, adult female

Arizona brown skink, juvenile

Variegated skink, adult male, breeding colors

128c. Variegated Skink, *P. g. cancellosus*, is the northwesternmost subspecies. It ranges southward from eastern San Francisco Bay to Monterey County. The tail of the juveniles is pink below and blue above. Adults may retain some striping.

128d. Adults of the Northern Brown Skink, *P. g. placerensis*, may retain vestiges of anterior striping. Juveniles have a blue tail. This subspecies ranges the farthest northward. It is a form of the Sierras and their foothills.

Northern brown skink, adult male, breeding colors

128e. The Western Red-tailed Skink, *P. g. rubricaudatus*, is strikingly beautiful. Juveniles have a bubblegum pink tail and the tail of the adults is suffused with red. Adults are most brightly colored during the breeding season. Although the name is descriptive of examples in most populations of this subspecies, a red tail is not restricted to this race alone. It is the southernmost race and occurs northward from interior northern Baja to Riverside and Kern counties, California.

Western red-tailed skink, adult male, breeding colors

Western red-tailed skink, hatchling

129. Northern Many-lined Skink

Plestiodon multivirgatus multivirgatus

Abundance/Range: This skink is not uncommon, but it is so secretive that it is seldom seen. It ranges southward from southern South Dakota to central eastern Colorado.

Habitat: This skink is pretty much a habitat generalist. It occurs in mountain meadows, lowland, mesquite-creosote bush, deserts, and, of course, intermediate areas. It prefers areas with ample rocky cover and is often found in the proximity of at least vestiges of moisture. It occurs also amid talus, in canyons, and in pine and oak woodland habitats. This skink ranges upward from 3,000 feet to 8,500 feet in elevation.

Northern Many-lined Skink
Plestiodon m. multivirgatus

Variable Skink
Plestiodon multivirgatus epipleurotus

Size: This very slender, noticeably attenuate skink is adult at 5½–7½ inches in total length. The tail is about 125% of the SVL. Hatchlings are about 2¼ inches in length.

Identifying features: This skink has the busiest pattern of any western species. It is primarily olive tan to olive buff with numerous light and dark stripes. The broad light middorsal area is flanked on each side by a heavy dark brown to black stripe. Below this the pattern is of wide or narrow

Northern many-lined skink

tan, black, white (or very light tan) stripes. The belly is light grayish tan. The tail of the adult is colored and patterned the same as body to near tip. Limbs are light in color.

Breeding males develop orange on the lips. Juveniles are very dark and bear 4 prominent light stripes.

Similar species: None in the west. In the east the short-lined skink may be confusing, but it is less elongate, lacks a dorsal stripe, and has the dorsolateral stripe restricted to the 4th row of scales from the midline. Hatchling Great Plains skinks are jet black on the trunk, have a very deep blue black tail, white or orange labial markings, and lateral scale rows diagonal to the dorsal rows.

ADDITIONAL SUBSPECIES

130. The more southerly Variable Skink, *P. m. epipleurotus*, has two distinctly different phases. Both may be produced in the same clutch. Ontogenetic changes are also apparent.

The dark many-striped phase has a broad olive brown vertebral area that is flanked by a black stripe on each side. Below this the pattern and colors are of olive brown, black, and tan stripes. The belly is sandy gray. The tail is bluish with rather obscure dark stripes anteriorly; the limbs are dark. Juveniles are very dark with 4 variably prominent light stripes, and with blue tails.

The light, or pallid, usually nonstriped phase, is an overall sandy buff or light gray. The hatchlings of this phase are nearly black with indistinct

Variable skink, both phases

striping. Some orange may be visible on the surface of the head and on the lips. The tail may be dark blue, but is often black. With growth, the ground color fades and the stripes become obscure.

The many-lined morph seems more common in moist, high-altitude habitats, while the nonstriped phase dominates lower, drier elevations.

131. Great Plains Skink

Plestiodon obsoletus

Abundance/Range: This is a common but seldom seen skink. It ranges from the western two-thirds of Texas to central Arizona, southern Nebraska, and extreme southwestern Iowa.

Habitat: This is one of the most secretive of the skinks. Despite its large size, it is adept at remaining hidden, even beneath comparatively small rocks or other surface debris. It is most common in rocky regions of grasslands, but also inhabits surrounding aridlands, trash piles, and dumps. It ranges in elevation from sea level to more than 8,500 feet.

Great Plains skink, adult

Great Plains skink, hatchling

Size: This is arguably the largest skink of the United States. With a record size of 13¾ inches, this species is a full inch longer that the reported record size for the runner-up, the more westerly brown skink. It is also heavy bodied. The tail of an adult is about 150% of the SVL. Hatchlings are about 2½ inches in length.

Identifying features: Juveniles of this large skink are easily described. The trunk is black, the tail is deep blue, and the black head is variably marked (most strongly on the labial scales) with orange or white. There is no striping. The adults are very different. They are tan, yellowish, buff, olive gray, to pale brown with variably sized dark flecks on the free edges of each scale. The upper labials are barred with black. The venter is yellow(ish). Breeding males develop a slight widening of the head and a vague suffusion of orange at the angle of the jaws. The lateral scale rows are diagonal to the dorsal and ventral rows. This latter is characteristic and unique to this species.

Similar species: No other western skink is similar to the adult. However, the juvenile of the variable skink is also nearly black in color but with poorly defined, orange dorsolateral stripes.

132. Skilton's Skink

Plestiodon skiltonianus skiltonianus

Abundance/Range: This is an abundant skink. When ground moisture levels are satisfactory it is easily found. When the ground dries it can be difficult to find. This race ranges southward from southern British Columbia, Canada, to western Nevada and southern California.

Habitat: This widespread skink utilizes a variety of habitats from sea level to 8,300 feet in elevation. Look for this species wherever there is surface debris for it to hide beneath. It may be found beneath rocks, logs, or trash in grasslands, pastures, woodland edges, sunny patches along forest trail edges, urban gardens, and other such locations.

Skilton's Skink
Plestiodon s. skiltonianus

Coronado Skink
Plestiodon s. interparietalis

Great Basin Skink
Plestiodon s. utahensis

Size: Although they may attain 9¼ inches in length, most adults are considerable smaller. The tail is slightly more than half the total length. Hatchlings are about 2¼ inches long.

Skilton's skink

Identifying features: The juveniles are strongly striped and have a very bright blue tail (rarely pinkish in a few populations). This is a 4-lined species. The back is warm brown, olive brown, or dark brown, palest in adults. There is a wide darker brown dorsolateral stripe on each side, from the ear opening to about halfway down the tail. This is bordered above and below by a thin yellow line. The upper yellow line is itself bordered by dark pigment. The stripes are retained throughout the life of the lizard. The belly is white. Males develop orange on the face during the breeding season. This is an oviparous species.

Similar species: Some color morphs of the Gilbert's skink can be confusingly similar to this species. Please see account 128.

ADDITIONAL SUBSPECIES

133. The Coronado Skink, *P. s. interparietalis*, is found from southern California to northern Baja. On this race the dark bands on the sides extend at least half the length of the tail.

Coronado skink

134. The light dorsolateral stripe of the Great Basin Skink, *P. s. utahensis*, of Idaho, Nevada, Utah, and extreme north central Arizona, is broad (half the width of the dark side stripe or greater) and usually lacks a dark upper border.

Great Basin skink

18

Whiptails and Racerunners

Family Teiidae

As a generality, the eastern forms of this family are referred to as racerunners, while those of the west are usually called whiptails.

Twenty species of whiptails occur in the western United States. None occur in Canada or the Hawaiian Islands. All whiptails are fast, nervous lizards. They routinely move in short bursts of speed. Most either construct home burrows (often beneath a rock or board) or utilize burrows made by other animals.

size of scales anterior to gular fold
help identify species

Whiptail throat showing gular fold

WHIPTAILS AND RACERUNNERS, GENUS *ASPIDOSCELIS*

Taxonomic note: In 2002 the generic name of *Aspidoscelis* was resurrected for the North American teiids that were, until then, in the genus *Cnemidophorus*.

Whiptails are active foragers that scratch through ground litter and loose sand to find their insect repast. Some readily eat plant materials. The lizards are confirmed heliotherms, basking between bouts of foraging. They tend to be most active from 9:00 in the morning to noontime but may forage well into the afternoon. All are terrestrial.

The dorsal and lateral scales of all racerunners and whiptails are small and evenly granular. The ventral scales are large and platelike and arranged in 8 parallel rows.

All whiptails are oviparous and several species are parthenogenetic. Ovulation is often stimulated by a pseudocourtship, and the unfertilized eggs then develop into clones of their mother.

Within a species, whiptails can be variable in appearance, hence difficult to identify. Among species in which males occur, they are larger, more brilliant, and easier to identify than the females.

There are three characteristics present on whiptails that often help with identification. These are the comparative size of the postantebrachial scales (scales on the rear of the forelimb), the size of the mesoptychial scales on the gular (throat) fold, and whether or not the supraorbital semicircles (small scales that outline the large scales above the eye) penetrate far anteriorly onto the snout.

A Bright-Throated Beauty

Ed Pirog and I walked quietly along "the flume." There is probably more than one flume in southern California, but to reptile enthusiasts this one was *the* flume, the long-dry but well-known water conveyance that entraps reptiles as diverse as blind snakes and rosy boas within its cemented walls.

But it was not the possibility of seeing snakes that had drawn us to the flume; rather, it was the possibility of seeing and photographing an orange-throated whiptail, *Aspidoscelis hyperythra beldingi*. Although not rare, this pretty whiptail is of spotty distribution.

And it was to be another of our lucky days, for we had hardly left our vehicle when we saw a little female—and only moments later had succeeded in photographing an adult male that was basking, stretched out so fully that it was almost flat, on the cement edge of the flume. Seldom is a photographic goal so easily attained!

135. Arizona Striped Whiptail

Aspidoscelis arizonae

Abundance/Range: This is a common (but perhaps declining) lizard of southeastern Arizona.
Habitat: Look for this species in grassland and sparsely vegetated desert habitats in low-elevation valleys.
Size: The total length is about 8¾ inches. SVL is 2¾–3 inches. Hatchlings are about 4 inches total.
Identifying features: This is a 7-striped whiptail. The lowest stripe on each side and the vertebral stripe are the least well defined. The back and sides are olive brown, brown, or reddish brown. The stripes are yellowish. There are no light spots between the stripes. The belly is light. There is usually a suffusion of pale blue on the throat, the sides of the face, the anterior aspect of all four limbs, the toes, and the sides of the belly. The distal two-thirds of the tail is a brighter blue.

Pregular fold (mesoptychial) scales: slightly enlarged.
Postantebrachials: slightly enlarged.
Supraorbital semicircles: do not penetrate forward.

Arizona striped whiptail. Photo by Randy Babb

Similar species: The little striped whiptail is very similar. See account 143. Also use ranges as diagnostic tools.

Comments: This pretty lizard was formerly a subspecies of *A. inornata*, the Little Striped Whiptail. Both sexes are present in this species.

ADDITIONAL SUBSPECIES

As currently recognized, none.

136. Giant Spotted Whiptail

Aspidoscelis burti stictogramma

Abundance/Range: Although predominantly a Mexican species, the giant spotted whiptail is relatively common within its limited range in southeastern Arizona and immediately adjacent New Mexico.

Habitat: This is a high canyon species that may be found in rocky grasslands and along streambeds.

Size: This is the largest whiptail in the western

Giant spotted whiptail

United States. It attains a total length of about 17 inches and a snout-vent length of approximately 5½ inches. Hatchlings are about 5½ inches in total length.

Identifying features: This is a huge, prominently spotted whiptail. If viewed from the side, the spots will appear to be haphazardly placed, but when seen from above the lizard's lineate pattern becomes obvious. Besides the spots, there are 6 or 7 variably visible light lines (the lowest line on each side and the vertebral strip are the most poorly defined). Adults have a straw yellow to brownish tail; the tail of juvenile examples is orangish. The throat and belly are white.

Pregular fold (mesoptychial) scales: prominently enlarged.

Postantebrachials: prominently enlarged.

Supraorbital semicircles: do not penetrate forward.

Similar species: All other whiptails within its range are much smaller than adult giant spotted whiptail.

Comments: Both sexes are present in this species.

ADDITIONAL SUBSPECIES

There are Mexican subspecies.

137. Gray-checkered Whiptail

Aspidoscelis dixoni

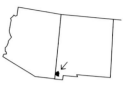

Abundance/Range: Although not an uncommon species, this whiptail is found in only two small areas, one in New Mexico and the other in western Texas. It has been suggested that the Texas population may be specifically distinct.

Habitat: This is a whiptail of rocky plains, dry washes, canyon bottoms, and desert scrub (ocotillo, creosote bush, opuntia).

Size: Large adults are between 10 and 12½ inches in total length. The tail is about 200% of the SVL. Hatchlings are about 4½ inches in total length.

Identifying features: Although clad in earthen hues, this is an attractive whiptail. The adults have a ground color of gray or grayish tan anteriorly. This shades to fawn near the hips. The dark lateral markings are vertically oriented. Dark dorsolateral markings are in 2 (or more) rows on each side of the irregular vertebral line. There are 10–14 poorly defined light lines on the back and sides. These lines are most visible anteriorly. Both the crown of the head and the tail are largely devoid of markings. The underside of the tail is light. The scales anterior to the gular fold are noticeably

Gray-checkered whiptail

enlarged. The limbs are mottled. There are no significantly enlarged scales on the posterior of the forearm. The light belly is sparingly marked with dark pigment. The chin is usually light in color and unmarked.

The hatchlings are prominently lineate—yellow on a black or dark brown ground.

Pre-gular fold (mesoptychial) scales: prominently enlarged.

Postantebrachials: not enlarged.

Supraorbital semicircles: penetrate anteriorly.

Similar species: The checkered whiptails, *A. tesselata* and *A. neotesselata*, are virtually identical in appearance to the gray-checkered whiptail, but may have a darker ground color and more contrasting pattern. Use the range maps when trying to identify these confusingly similar lizards.

Comments: This is a unisexual, all female (parthenogenetic) species. This species was derived from hybridization between the marbled whiptail and the plateau spotted whiptail.

138. Chihuahuan Spotted Whiptail

Aspidoscelis exsanguis

Abundance/Range: This Trans-Pecos lizard is a habitat generalist. It occurs in west Texas, then beyond through southern New Mexico, to southeastern Arizona and northern Mexico. It is of common occurrence.

Habitat: A whiptail of wooded hillsides, rocky plains, grasslands, dry washes, canyon bottoms, and desert scrub (ocotillo, creosote bush, opuntia), this fast and alert lizard can be very difficult to approach.

Size: The total length of large adults varies between 10 and 12¼ inches. The tail is greater than 200% of the SVL. Hatchlings may exceed 5 inches in total length.

Identifying features: This is a dark whiptail with a busy pattern of (usually) 6 lighter stripes overlain with even lighter spots in both the light and dark fields. The ground color is dark brown to brownish gray. The stripes are pale cream to pale yellow, the spots are brighter. The paravertebral stripes are separated by 5–8 scale rows and, because of the placement of the lighter spots, often appear wavy. Younger lizards have a darker ground and more contrasting yellows than old adults. The light belly is usually

Chihuahuan spotted whiptail

devoid of dark pigment but may have a faint blush of blue. The chin is usually light in color and unmarked. The tail is gray, brown, or greenish.

The hatchlings are prominently lineate—yellow on a black or dark brown ground.

Pre-gular fold (mesoptychial) scales: greatly enlarged.

Postantebrachials: greatly enlarged.

Supraorbital semicircles: do not penetrate anteriorly.

Similar species: The Texas spotted whiptail is confusingly similar, but often has 8 stripes, a reddish (rather than a gray or brown) tail, and light spots largely restricted to dark fields. The New Mexican whiptail has a vividly contrasting pattern. Little striped whiptail and plateau striped whiptail lack spots.

Comments: This is an all-female (parthenogenetic) species. This whiptail has a lengthy lineage of complex hybridization. Genetic research has disclosed that its parental species comprise the little striped whiptail, (probably) the giant whiptail, and the plateau spotted whiptail.

ADDITIONAL SUBSPECIES

None.

139. Gila Spotted Whiptail

Aspidoscelis flagellicauda

Abundance/Range: This is a fairly common whiptail that occurs in the Gila River drainage of central Arizona and immediately adjacent New Mexico. It occurs also in the Catalina and the Chiricahua mountains of southeastern Arizona.

Habitat: This is a whiptail of open pine-juniper-oak woodlands, of montane meadow edges, and of chaparral. It can be particularly common in the proximity of intermittent streams and is found at elevations between 4,000 and 6,500 feet.

Size: This whiptail is adult at 10–12½ inches in total length. The tail is about three times the SVL. Hatchlings are almost 5 inches long.

Identifying features: This 6-striped whiptail has light spots both in the dark fields and in the light stripes. The light stripes are a bright yellow on the neck but fade in intensity at the shoulders. The throat and belly are white or have a vague bluish tinge. The tail is usually olive tan but may be vaguely tinged with blue. Juveniles have light spots on the trunk.

Gila spotted whiptail

Pre-gular fold (mesoptychial) scales: prominently enlarged.

Postantebrachials: prominently enlarged.

Supraorbital semicircles: do not penetrate anteriorly.

Similar species: The desert grassland whiptail lacks spots. The stripes of the Chihuahuan spotted whiptail are not brighter on the neck than the body.

Comments: This is an all-female (parthenogenetic) species.

ADDITIONAL SUBSPECIES

None.

140. Texas Spotted Whiptail

Aspidoscelis gularis gularis

Abundance/Range: This whiptail species enters our region only in southeastern New Mexico but it is common to the east and south. It is also found through most of Texas, adjacent southern Oklahoma, and northern Mexico.

Habitat: The Texas spotted whiptail is found in gravelly, sandy areas. It is most common where there is a

Texas spotted whiptail

sparse cover of low herbs and shrubs and is commonly seen near nature centers, park buildings, and other such habitations. Rocky hillsides, grasslands, rocky washes, and road cuts are also favored habitats.

Size: This is a moderately large and fairly robust whiptail. Large males may attain 10½ inches in total length. Females are fully grown at 7½–8½ inches. The tail is nearly twice as long as the SVL. Hatchlings are about 4 inches in total length.

Identifying features: This is a very colorful lizard. It may have either 7 or, if the vertebral stripe is narrowly divided, 8 stripes. The ground color can vary from a warm brown to a rather dark brown. The stripes may vary from nearly white to yellow to pale green. The two lowermost dark side stripes are liberally marked with light spots. During the breeding season males develop a pink to pinkish orange throat. The venter may either have a black area surrounded by blue or be entirely blue. The tail may be orange brown to reddish. Females are smaller, and have light venters (including chin). Hatchlings have yellow stripes on a black ground, poorly defined lateral spots, and a rather bright reddish tail.

Pre-gular fold (mesoptychial) scales: prominently enlarged.

Postantebrachials: not enlarged.

Supraorbital semicircles: do not penetrate anteriorly.

Similar species: No related lizard within the range of the Texas spotted whiptail bears the same suite of colors borne by the male Texas spotted whiptail. Females are a bit more confusing.

Comments: This is a bisexual whiptail.

141. Little White Whiptail

Aspidoscelis gypsi

Abundance/Range: Although rather common, this whiptail is restricted in distribution to only two New Mexico counties, Dona Ana and Otero.

Habitat: This species is known only from sparsely vegetated white sand dunes.

Size: This is a small whiptail species. Adult males attain only 9½ inches in total length. The very long tail can near 300% of the SVL. Hatchlings are about 3½ inches in total length.

Identifying features: This is a pale but beautiful whiptail. The back and

Little white whiptail

sides are light, and the striping is very pale. The head, tail, and lower sides are a robin's egg blue. Juveniles are paler than the adults. Other keynote features:

Pre-gular fold (mesoptychial) scales: slightly enlarged.

Postantebrachials: slightly enlarged.

Supraorbital semicircles: do not penetrate forward.

Similar species: None.

Comments: This species was long considered a subspecies of the little striped whiptail.

ADDITIONAL SUBSPECIES

As currently understood, none.

142. Belding's Orange-throated Whiptail

Aspidoscelis hyperythra beldingi

Abundance/Range: Although still common in some areas, this whiptail is dramatically reduced in numbers over vast sections of its range.

Habitat: Rocky hillsides vegetated with sparse desert scrub, coastal chaparral, thornscrub, and the environs of intermittent streams.

Size: Adult males attain 7–10½ inches in total length; females are an inch or so smaller.

Belding's orange-throated whiptail, male

Belding's orange-throated whiptail, male

Identifying features: We finally have a whiptail on which the males may be easily identified by their orange throat and chest. The underside of the otherwise blue gray tail may also be orange. The orange highlights are brightest during the breeding season. There are 5 (more rarely 6) light lines on the brown body. The belly is white. Females lack the orange highlights but are otherwise similar to the male.

Pre-gular fold (mesoptychial) scales: not enlarged.

Postantebrachials: not enlarged.

Supraorbital semicircles: do not penetrate anteriorly.

Similar species: The tiger whiptail has prominent spots and bars on the sides and back and lacks an orange throat.

Comments: This is a bisexual species.

ADDITIONAL SUBSPECIES

Other subspecies of questionable validity occur in Mexico.

143. Little Striped Whiptail

Aspidoscelis inornata ssp.

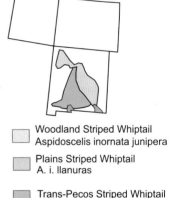

Taxonomic comment: *Aspidoscelis inornata*, a very variable whiptail species, is represented by three very similar appearing (and questionably valid) subspecies in the southwestern United States. The three often have overlapping characteristics. Use range as the primary identifying feature.

Abundance/Range: This is a commonly encountered whiptail. It occurs in western Texas and throughout most of New Mexico. It ranges well southward into Mexico.

Woodland Striped Whiptail
Aspidoscelis inornata junipera

Plains Striped Whiptail
A. i. llanuras

Trans-Pecos Striped Whiptail
A. i. heptagramma

Habitat: Look for this whiptail in desert grasslands, on rocky hillsides, amid low vegetation along dry washes, and in other such areas. Usually associated with rocky habitats, it may occasionally be seen in sandy areas.

Size: This is a small whiptail species. Adult males attain only 9½ inches in total length. The very long tail can near 300% of the SVL. Hatchlings are about 3½ inches in total length.

Identifying features: This is a prominently striped, nonspotted whiptail. It normally has 7 (sometimes 8) cream to yellow stripes against a very dark ground color, or, rarely, no stripes. The tail is quite a bright blue. Males have a rather bright blue belly and chin and a brighter tail than the females. Females have a pale blue belly and chin. Hatchlings have bright yellow stripes and a pale blue tail.

Pregular fold (mesoptychial) scales: slightly enlarged.

Postantebrachials: slightly enlarged.

Supraorbital semicircles: do not penetrate forward.

Similar species: Desert grassland whiptail and New Mexican whiptail have pale bluish green tails. The New Mexican whiptail has a wavy vertebral stripe. The range of the prairie racerunner does not near that of the little striped whiptail.

Comments: This whiptail has been shown to be a parent species in several of the parthenogenetic hybrid species of whiptails!

ADDITIONAL SUBSPECIES

143a. The Trans-Pecos Striped Whiptail, *Aspidoscelis inornata heptagramma*, ranges westward from Texas' Trans-Pecos region to southern southwestern New Mexico.

Trans-Pecos striped whiptail

Woodland striped whiptail

143b. The Woodland Striped Whiptail, *Aspidoscelis inornata junipera*, occurs in suitable habitat from central New Mexico to northwestern New Mexico.

143c. The Plains Striped Whiptail, *Aspidoscelis inornata llanuras*, occurs from north central to southwestern New Mexico.

Plains striped whiptail

144. Western Marbled Whiptail

Aspidoscelis marmorata marmorata

Abundance/Range: This is a common species through the western Trans-Pecos, central New Mexico, and northern Mexico.

Habitat: This is a species of sparsely vegetated (ocotillo, creosote bush, opuntia) sandy desert.

Size: Large adults may measure up to 12 inches in total length. The tail is about 275% of the SVL. Hatchlings measure about 5 inches in total length.

Identifying features: This common desert lizard is variably patterned. Typically the adults have a ground color of brownish tan to brown. The markings, when present, are only a few shades darker than the ground color and, although of variable shape, are precisely delineated. The dark lateral markings are vertically oriented. Dark dorsal markings may have squared corners, but are more often rounded and arranged as a reticulum. The limbs are reticulated on the upper surface, and the tail is of the ground color and is unmarked. The belly is light posteriorly, light

Western marbled whiptail

with darker markings anteriorly; the dark-spotted chin and throat are peach to salmon in color.

The hatchlings are prominently lineate—pale spots on a dark ground color—and have a tail of variable blue.

Pre-gular fold (mesoptychial) scales: slightly enlarged.

Postantebrachials: not enlarged.

Supraorbital semicircles: extend far forward.

Similar species: The Chihuahuan spotted whiptail has a patch of enlarged scales on the rear of each forelimb and along the anterior edge of the gular fold. The common checkered whiptail and the gray checkered whiptail have greatly enlarged anterior gular throat scales. Despite these differences, determining an exact identification can be most exasperating.

Comments: This big whiptail is one of the few lizards that may be out and actively foraging on the hottest of summer days. At such times it remains close to cover, but as if aware that its speed and agility will afford safety, it may dart out into the open if approached. This is one of the wariest of the whiptails. Both sexes are present in this species.

ADDITIONAL SUBSPECIES

None in the west.

145. New Mexican Whiptail

Aspidoscelis neomexicana

Abundance/Range: This common whiptail ranges from Presidio County, Texas, to central northern New Mexico.

Habitat: This species is found in city parks, cemeteries, suburban neighborhoods, campuses, and sandy washes.

Size: This whiptail is of moderate adult size. Adults are most often between 8 and 10 inches in length (including a tail that may be slightly longer than 300% of the SVL) but may occasionally attain 12 inches total length.

Identifying features: This long-tailed whiptail has a brownish ground color and 7 light stripes. There are light spots in the lateral and dorsolat-

New Mexican whiptail

eral dark fields. The vertebral stripe (and occasionally the paravertebral stripes) is wavy. The venter is often an immaculate white but may have a blue wash. The brownish tail is a pale greenish blue distally. Hatchlings have a tail of rather bright blue. This fades to the adult color rather quickly with growth. The limbs are mottled. The chin is usually bluish.

Pregular fold (mesoptychial) scales: not enlarged

Postantebrachials: not enlarged.

Supraorbital semicircles: penetrate far forward.

Similar species: Eliminate some of the look-alike species by range. The little striped whiptail retains a decidedly blue tail throughout its life and has no spotting in the dark fields. The Chihuahuan spotted whiptail is *prominently* spotted. The desert grassland whiptail has no spots in the dark fields. The Texas spotted whiptail has well-defined spots laterally, and males have a pink throat.

Comments: This is a unisexual, all-female (parthenogenetic) species. This species was derived from hybridization of the little striped whiptail and the marbled whiptail.

ADDITIONAL SUBSPECIES

None.

146. Colorado Checkered Whiptail

Aspidoscelis neotesselata

Abundance/Range: This is a locally distributed, relatively common whiptail from southeastern Colorado.

Habitat: Expect this lizard in sparsely vegetated canyons, on prairies, and even near country homesteads.

Size: This pretty lizard attains the length of 12 inches or slightly more. Hatchlings are about 5 inches long.

Identifying features: Range will be an important identifying tool. It is primarily through genetics that this lizard is separated from the more southerly common checkered whiptail. The two are of very similar appearance. The 7 or, if the vertebral stripe is split, 8 stripes are grayish. Many of the light spots touch the stripes. The sides are patterned with vertical bars. The belly is light and may or may not be patterned with dark spots. The grayish tail is spotted.

Colorado checkered whiptail

Pre-gular fold (mesoptychial) scales: prominently enlarged.

Postantebrachials: not enlarged.

Supraorbital semicircles: penetrate anteriorly.

Similar species: There are no other whiptails within the range of this species.

Comments: This is an all-female, parthenogenetic species. It was long considered a triploid variant of the common checkered whiptail. The Colorado checkered whiptail is derived from the hybridization of the common checkered whiptail (itself a hybrid) and the prairie racerunner.

ADDITIONAL SUBSPECIES

None.

147. Pai Striped Whiptail

Aspidoscelis pai

Abundance/Range: This is a commonly encountered whiptail. It is found in northern Arizona and in the Mazatzal mountains in central Arizona.

Habitat: This whiptail is usually associated with rocky areas in habitats as diverse as grasslands and montane pine forests.

Size: This is a small whiptail species. Adult males attain only 9½ inches in total length. The very long tail can near 300% of the SVL. Hatchlings are about 3½ inches in total length.

Identifying features: Range alone will separate this species from several look-alike forms. This is a prominently striped, nonspotted whiptail. It has 6 cream to yellow stripes against an olive brown to brown ground color. The stripes are most vivid anteriorly. The tail is quite a bright blue. Males have a rather bright blue belly and chin and a brighter tail than the females. Females have a pale blue belly and chin. Hatchlings have bright yellow stripes and a pale blue tail.

Pregular fold (mesoptychial) scales: slightly enlarged.

Postantebrachials: slightly enlarged.

Supraorbital semicircles: do not penetrate forward.

Pai striped whiptail

Similar species: Desert grassland whiptail has a pale bluish green tail. The blue of the plateau striped whiptail is paler. The Gila spotted whiptail is prominently spotted.

Comments: This whiptail has been shown to be a parent species in several of the parthenogenetic hybrid species of whiptails!

148. Prairie Racerunner

Aspidoscelis sexlineata viridis

Abundance/Range: This is a common lizard. It ranges westward from northern Indiana to eastern New Mexico and Wyoming.

Habitat: The prairie racerunner is a species of well-drained sandy fields, scrub, sandy parking lot edges, and myriad other such habitats.

Size: This is a small teiid. Adult males attain 7–10½ inches in total length; females are an inch or so smaller. The tail is 225% of the SVL or longer. Hatchlings are nearly 3 inches in total length.

Prairie racerunner

Identifying features: This is the most brightly colored and westerly ranging subspecies of this group. Breeding males are suffused over nearly their entire body with a flush of green, brightest laterally and especially so on the sides of the neck. The green is more reduced, both in intensity and quantity, on nonbreeding males and on females. The 6 lines from which the nominate form takes its name are brightly distinct. Additionally a single pale vertebral stripe, which is sometimes narrowly divided centrally into 2, is present. The darkest field of color on each side is between the paravertebral and the dorsolateral stripe.

Gular fold: greatly enlarged.

Postantebrachials: only moderately enlarged or not enlarged.

Supraorbital semicircles: do not extend far forward.

Similar species: Range and color should identify this racerunner (whiptail). Immature skinks have shiny mirrorlike scales.

Comment: Both sexes are present in this species.

ADDITIONAL SUBSPECIES

There are two additional more easterly subspecies.

149. Sonoran Spotted Whiptail

Aspidoscelis sonorae

Abundance/Range: This common whiptail occurs in southeastern Arizona and immediately adjacent New Mexico. It is also found southward to central Sonora, Mexico.

Sonoran spotted whiptail

Habitat: This whiptail prefers grasslands and open oak woodlands with ample sunny patches. It ranges in elevation from 700 to nearly 7,000 feet, but is seemingly more common at the higher elevations.

Size: Large adults of this whiptail are about 11½ inches long. The tails is about 275% of the SVL. Hatchlings are about 4½ inches in total length.

Identifying features: This strongly patterned whiptail has both prominent stripes and rows of discrete spots. There are 6 stripes, occasionally 7 on neck. The spots are present only in the olive brown to fawn dark fields. The upper surface of the hind legs is mottled. The tail may have a pale orange flush but is usually grayish distally. The belly and throat are off-white. Hatchlings lack light spots.

Pre-gular fold (mesoptychial) scales: prominently enlarged.

Postantebrachials: prominently enlarged.

Supraorbital semicircles: do not penetrate anteriorly.

Similar species: The light stripes of the Chihuahuan spotted whiptail are very faint on the neck. The Gila spotted whiptail has a greenish tail.

Comments: This is an all-female, parthenogenetic species. The genetics of this whiptail are complicated and remain unresolved. This taxon may actually be a species complex that contains several undescribed species.

ADDITIONAL SUBSPECIES

None.

150. Common Checkered Whiptail

Aspidoscelis tesselata

Abundance/Range: This common species occurs in west Texas, most of New Mexico, and a tiny range in extreme southeastern Colorado.

Habitat: This is a whiptail of rocky plains, dry washes, canyon bottoms, floodplains, and rocky areas of desert scrub.

Size: The total length of large adults ranges from 12 inches to 15½ inches. The tail is very long, often nearing 300% of the SVL. Hatchlings are about 5 inches long.

Identifying features: This beautiful lizard is clad in a ground color of tan, yellowish, cream, or gray and may be strikingly patterned with vertically oriented lateral bars and have paired or entire heavy dorsal crossbars, or may be finely peppered with longitudinal rows of black or dark brown spots. Light stripes are present and may number from as few as 6 to as many as 14. The venter is either light and immaculate or may bear some dark spotting. The tail is spotted, most prominently on the sides. Despite its somber colors, this is an attractive whiptail. The scales anterior to the gular fold are noticeably enlarged. The limbs are mottled. There are no significantly enlarged scales on the posterior of the forearm. The chin is usually light in color and unmarked.

The hatchlings are prominently lineate—yellow on a black or dark brown ground.

Pre-gular fold (mesoptychial) scales: prominently enlarged.

Postantebrachials: not enlarged.

Supraorbital semicircles: penetrate anteriorly.

Similar species: The marbled whiptail has a dark-spotted peach-colored chin, and the scales anterior to the gular fold are only moderately enlarged. The Chihuahuan spotted whiptail has a patch of enlarged scales on the rear of each forelimb, and the underside of the tail is dark. The gray-checkered whiptail occurs only in Hidalgo County, New Mexico, and Presidio County, Texas. It is virtually identical in appearance to the checkered whiptail, but may have a lighter ground color and a more contrasting pattern. Use range extensively when trying to identify these confusingly similar lizards.

Comments: This hybrid lizard originated from the pairing of the marbled

Common checkered whiptail

whiptail and the plateau spotted whiptail. It is an all-female, parthenogenetic species.

ADDITIONAL SUBSPECIES

None.

151. Great Basin Whiptail

Aspidoscelis tigris tigris

Abundance/Range: This is an abundant whiptail with a huge range. It occurs from Idaho and eastern Oregon southward through the Great Basin to northern Baja California and Sonora, Mexico.

Habitat: Deserts and semideserts are the macrohabitats. In these it may inhabit the edges of grasslands, boulder fields, sagebrush, and thornscrub. It is often found along intermittent streams, near desert springs, and around stock tanks.

Size: The races in the United States top out at about 12½ inches in total length. The tail is about 300% of the SVL. Hatchlings measure about 5 inches in total length.

Identifying features: The back usually has 4 rather poorly defined light stripes. Dark vertical bars are present on the sides. The hind limbs are marked with dark spots or a complex reticulum. The belly may be an immaculate off-white or heavily spotted. Hatchlings are black with yellow stripes and a blue tail.

Pre-gular fold (mesoptychial) scales: slightly enlarged.

Postantebrachials: not enlarged.

Supraorbital semicircles: extend far forward.

Similar species: See the accounts for the common checkered whiptail (150), the gray-checkered whiptail (137), and the Colorado checkered whiptail (146).

Comments: Although both sexes of this whiptail are known, in some populations males may be absent or quite uncommon.

California Whiptail
Aspidoscelis tigris munda

Coastal Whiptail
Aspidoscelis t. stejnegeri

Great Basin Whiptail
Aspidoscelis t. tigris

Plateau Tiger Whiptail
Aspidoscelis t. septentrionalis

Sonoran Desert Whiptail
Aspidoscelis t. punctilinealis

Great Basin whiptail

ADDITIONAL SUBSPECIES

152. The California Tiger Whiptail, *Aspidoscelis tigris munda*, is pale in overall coloration. Eight light stripes are usually present, with the lateral lines being the most poorly defined. Lateral barring is usually pale or even absent. The throat is pale, but dark spots are usually present. This race occurs in northern and central California.

California tiger whiptail

153. The Sonoran Tiger Whiptail, *Aspidoscelis tigris punctilinealis*, usually has 6 light stripes, but all are variably prominent. The lateral pair is the least well defined. Dorsal and lateral markings tend to be spots rather than bars. The throat and chest are usually quite dark. This race is found from central Arizona and immediately adjacent central western New Mexico to central Sonora, Mexico.

Sonoran tiger whiptail

Plateau tiger whiptail

154. The Plateau Tiger Whiptail, *Aspidoscelis tigris septentrionalis*, is very similar in appearance to the Sonoran race. The dorsal striping tends to be more vivid and the stripes often stop on the lower back. This is the High Plains race. It is found from the vicinity of the Four Corners to northwestern Arizona and southwestern Utah.

155. The Coastal Tiger Whiptail, *Aspidoscelis tigris stejnegeri*, is quite similar in appearance to the California tiger whiptail. However, the lateral striping is pale and poorly defined, and the throat tends to be dark. This race ranges southward from Riverside County, California, to northern Baja, Mexico.

Coastal whiptail

156. Desert Grassland Whiptail

Aspidoscelis uniparens

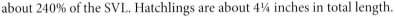

Abundance/Range: This abundant whiptail is found in northern Mexico, New Mexico, Arizona, and extreme western Texas.

Habitat: As its common name indicates, this is a whiptail of the desert grasslands and associated scrub.

Size: With an adult length of only 9½ inches, this is one of the smaller species of whiptails. The tail is about 240% of the SVL. Hatchlings are about 4¼ inches in total length.

Identifying features: This is a quietly colored, prominently striped, nonspotted whiptail. It has 6 (rarely 7) yellow stripes against a very dark ground color. Hatchlings resemble the adults but have a tail of rather bright blue. This fades with age and usually becomes tinged with green. This bluish green tinge persists throughout the life of the lizard. The limbs are mottled. The belly is white and unmarked. The chin is usually bluish.

Pregular fold (mesoptychial) scales: enlarged.

Postantebrachials: enlarged.

Supraorbital semicircles: do not penetrate anteriorly.

Similar species: The little striped whiptail retains a decidedly blue tail throughout its life. The New Mexico whiptail has a wavy vertebral stripe. The range of the six-lined racerunner does not near that of the desert grassland whiptail. The prairie racerunner is usually tinged with green.

Desert grassland whiptail

Comments: This is a unisexual, all-female (parthenogenetic) species. The parental species of this small hybrid whiptail have not yet been satisfactorily resolved.

ADDITIONAL SUBSPECIES

None.

157. Plateau Striped Whiptail

Aspidoscelis velox

Abundance/Range: This common whiptail has the Four Corners region as the center of its large range.
Habitat: This species occurs in clearings in open pine-oak-juniper woodlands and plateau brushlands. It ranges in elevation between 3,900 and 8,000 feet.
Size: Adults are between 8 and 11 inches in total length. The tail is about 250% of the SVL. Hatchlings are about 4½ inches in length.
Identifying features: This prominently striped whiptail has few if any spots. It has 6–7 light dorsal stripes, with the vertebral stripe the least visible and occasionally absent. The chin is blue; the belly is white or very

Plateau striped whiptail

pale blue. The tail is decidedly blue. Hatchlings are darker than the adults and have very well-defined stripes and a bright blue tail.

Pre-gular fold (mesoptychial) scales: prominently enlarged.

Postantebrachials: enlarged.

Supraorbital semicircles: do not penetrate anteriorly.

Similar species: Most other whiptails within the range of this species are conspicuously spotted. The little striped whiptail is smaller when adult and lacks conspicuously enlarged scales on the gular fold and the rear of the forelimbs.

Comments: This is a unisexual, all-female (parthenogenetic) species. The parental species of this small hybrid whiptail have not yet been satisfactorily resolved.

ADDITIONAL SUBSPECIES

None.

158. Red-backed Whiptail

Aspidoscelis xanthonota

Abundance/Range: The canyon-dwelling red-backed whiptail is relatively common but spottily distributed. It occurs in south central Arizona and perhaps in adjacent Sonora, Mexico.

Habitat: This is a high canyon species that may be found in rocky grasslands and along streambeds.

Size: This whiptail attains a length of about 13 inches (but most are smaller). The tail is about 275% of the SVL. Hatchlings are about 5 inches in total length.

Identifying features: This is a large rather whiptail with a distinctive reddish back. The red dorsal color largely obscures the dorsal spotting. Spotting is present on the reddish tan sides. Besides the spots there may be 6 or 7 obscure lines. Adults have a grayish tail; the tail of juvenile examples is orangish. The throat and belly are off-white.

Pregular fold (mesoptychial) scales: prominently enlarged.

Postantebrachials: prominently enlarged.

Supraorbital semicircles: do not penetrate forward.

Similar species: No other whiptail has a reddish back.

Red-backed whiptail

Comments: Both sexes are present in this species. This whiptail was long considered a subspecies of the giant spotted whiptail.

ADDITIONAL SUBSPECIES

None.

19

Night Lizards

Family Xantusiidae

This family contains three genera of small lizards. One genus occurs in Cuba, another in mainland Mexico and Central America, and the third in the western United States, the Baja Peninsula, and central mainland Mexico.

Like the geckos, the night lizards have lidless eyes covered by a transparent spectacle (the brille) and vertical pupils. Night lizards do not have flattened toepads. Many species are associated with granitic outcrops and boulders while others dwell beneath and in the leaf axils of fallen yuccas.

NIGHT LIZARDS, GENUS *XANTUSIA*

Many species in this genus are so small, secretive, and cryptically colored that they are very easily overlooked.

Dorsal and lateral scales are tiny and granular. The ventral scales are larger, platelike, and in 12 or 14 rows, except for the Island night lizards, which have 16 rows. Large smooth scales are also present on the head. The caudal scales form rings (annuli).

A gular fold is present and a lateral fold runs from the apex of the forelimb to the groin.

One to 4 (up to 9 for the Island night lizards) comparatively large live babies are produced by the females toward the end of the summer.

All are thought to eat insects and spiders. The Island night lizards are known to also eat some vegetable matter.

Despite the common name bestowed on this lizard group, at least some of the species are diurnally active.

An Island Dweller

A chilly wind and California sea lions greeted us, thirty visitors egressing the bobbing boat at the dock. We all climbed the steep set of steps chiseled into the access route, and most of us arrived gasping for breath at the visitor's center of Channel Island National Park on Santa Barbara Island, California. The trip over had been exciting. We had seen thousands of common porpoises, myriad seabirds of dozens of species, and a blue whale. How much better can things possibly be for naturalists, be they casual or professional? Now, above us, gulls, ever alert for food, rode the air currents, mewling plaintively in hopes that someone would turn their back for a moment on a picnic lunch.

Giant coreopsis and other plants, most of them seasonally devoid of leaves, edged the trails. We walked slowly to the picnic area hoping against hope to see an island night lizard, *Xantusia riversiana*. Like many xantusiids, this species is actually active by both day and night. However, since the species is endemic to only three of the Channel Islands, all either national park or under military control, it is not an easy lizard to see. Yet it was exactly this, the hope of seeing this creature, that had drawn us to this remote location.

The day was cool, the island not yet warmed by a sun that shown only fitfully through a pervasive layer of sea fog. I gathered my jacket more tightly about me. Would we be lucky? Would a night lizard actually be out on this kind of day? The answer was quick in coming.

The sun peeked through for a few moments, illuminating ground and rocks, and on the sloping side of one small rock there was a juvenile night lizard. We were lucky, very lucky. But we were soon to be even luckier, for just a bit away from the picnicking crowd, on a flat rock surrounded by grasses and prickly pear cactus, lay a stocky, full-grown adult that allowed us an opportunity to get photos. Still early, the day had already been a complete and, although hoped for, almost unexpected success.

159. Arizona Night Lizard

Xantusia arizonae

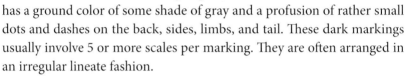

Abundance/Range: This is a fairly common night lizard along the Mogollon Rim in Arizona.

Habitat: This is one of the saxicolous night lizards. It is found in boulder fields and outcroppings.

Size: Total length is 4¼ inches. The tail is 150% of the SVL. Neonates are about 2 inches in length.

Identifying features: This is another of the some-what flattened crevice-dwelling night lizards. It has a ground color of some shade of gray and a profusion of rather small dots and dashes on the back, sides, limbs, and tail. These dark markings usually involve 5 or more scales per marking. They are often arranged in an irregular lineate fashion.

Similar species: Bezy's night lizard is found only near Sunflower, Arizona, and has much larger dark spots.

Comments: Many researchers continue to consider this lizard a subspecies of the yucca night lizard. It is then listed as *Xantusia vigilis arizonae*. This species has a diurnal and crepuscular activity pattern.

ADDITIONAL SUBSPECIES

As currently understood, none.

Arizona night lizard

160. Bezy's Night Lizard

Xantusia bezyi

Abundance/Range: This lizard is fairly common in its specific, localized, and restricted habitat. It is known to occur only in the vicinity of Sunflower, Maricopa County, Arizona.

Habitat: This saxicolous species may be found behind granite flakes as well as in crevices and between loosened rock sections in boulder fields and outcroppings.

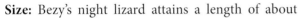

Size: Bezy's night lizard attains a length of about 4½ inches. The tail is slightly longer than the SVL. Neonates are about 2 inches long.

Identifying features: This is a rather long-legged, somewhat flattened lizard. The ground color is of some shade of gray, with a profusion of large black spots of irregular shape randomly scattered over it.

Similar species: Arizona night lizard has smaller dark blotches, often in a lineate pattern.

Comment: This species has a diurnal and crepuscular activity pattern.

ADDITIONAL SUBSPECIES

None.

Bezy's night lizard

161. Sandstone Night Lizard

Xantusia gracilis

Abundance/Range: Very little is known about this night lizard, but it does not seem to be uncommon. It is found only on and in the immediate environs of a single sandstone outcropping. Because of their restricted distribution, the populations are vulnerable. It is known only from Truckhaven Rocks in Anza Borrego State Park, California.

Habitat: This lizard shelters in flakes, breaks, and crevices in a single sandstone prominence.

Size: An adult size of 5½ inches is attained by this species. Neonates are about 2 inches long.

Identifying features: Like other rock-dwelling night lizards, this species is wary, secretive, and agile. It is long legged and flattened. The dorsal and lateral ground color is grayish tan to light gray. The dorsal spots are small and contrast sharply with the ground color. The belly is light but may have sparse dark markings. A gular fold and a lateral fold are both present.

Similar species: Granite night lizard has small to large, but always promi-

Sandstone night lizard

nent dark dorsal spots, and many dark markings on the belly, and it is capable of considerable color change.

Comments: Some researchers continue to consider this a subspecies of the granite night lizard (as it was initially described). Its scientific nomenclature is then *Xantusia henshawi gracilis*.

ADDITIONAL SUBSPECIES

None.

162. Granite Night Lizard

Xantusia henshawi

Abundance/Range: This is an abundant but very secretive lizard of southwestern California and adjacent Baja California.

Habitat: This lizard shelters in flakes, breaks, and crevices in granite boulders and escarpments. It is also known to colonize the walls of dwellings, bridge abutments, caves, and other darkened areas of seclusion.

Size: This slender night lizard attains an adult size of 5½ inches. Neonates are about 2 inches long.

Granite night lizard

Identifying features: This wary and agile night lizard becomes active at dusk and forages long after darkness has fallen. It is long legged and flattened. The dorsal and lateral ground color is grayish tan, light gray, or dark gray. An individual lizard is capable of undergoing rapid changes of the ground color (metachrosis). When exposed to the light, the dark dorsal spots may be small and discrete and contrast sharply with the widened areas of ground color. When the lizard is in a darkened area the areas of ground color darken, narrow noticeably, and blend well with the dark blotches. The belly is light with many dark markings. A gular fold and a lateral fold are both present.

Similar species: Sandstone night lizard is found only on Truckhaven Rocks in Anza Borrego State Park, southern California. It has very sparse dark markings on the light venter.

ADDITIONAL SPECIES

None.

163. San Nicolas Island Night Lizard

Xantusia riversiana riversiana

Abundance/Range: Common, but of restricted distribution, this large night lizard is found on San Nicolas Island in California's Channel Islands. It is a protected species.

Habitat: This lizard is found beneath rocks, boards, and other surface cover. It seems to be primarily active by day, but also forages in the early evening and is know to be active shortly after nightfall.

San Nicolas Night Lizard
Xantusia riversiana riversiana

San Clemente Night Lizard
Xantusia riversiana reticulata

Size: Although most are adult at a length of 5–6 inches, this, the largest of the night lizards of the United

San Nicolas night lizard. Photo by Gary M. Fellers

States, may attain a length of 8½ inches. Neonates are a bit less than 3 inches long.

Identifying features: The ground color may be gray, brown, yellowish, tan, or reddish. There may or may not be black blotches or reticulations. A pair of broken or solid light dorsolateral stripes may be present. These may extend onto the base of the tail or discontinue at midbody. There are 16 rows of belly scales and 2 rows of supraocular scales. A gular fold and a lateral fold are both present.

Similar species: None on the Channel Islands. The alligator lizard, present on the Channel Islands, has large, *shiny*, dorsal scales.

ADDITIONAL SUBSPECIES

164. The populations of this night lizard on Santa Barbara, San Clemente, and Isla Sutil, Channel Islands, California are occasionally given subspecific status and referred to as the San Clemente Night Lizard, *Xantusia riversiana reticulata*. There is a slight, but seemingly not consistent, difference in the number of longitudinal scale rows between the night lizards in these populations and those on San Nicolas. Use range to differentiate the two.

San Clemente night lizard

San Clemente night lizard, striped phase. Photo by Jeff Lemm

165. Sierra Night Lizard

Xantusia sierrae

Abundance/Range: Although it is common, the presence of this tiny secretive lizard is often unsuspected. It seemingly occurs only in the immediate vicinity of Granite Station, California.

Habitat: A "flake and fissure form," this night lizard may be found beneath granite flakes, in fissures, and beneath isolated rocks.

Size: Adults are seldom more than 3½ inches in length, of which the tail length is slightly more than half. Neonates are almost 2 inches in length.

Identifying features: This is an agile and fast-moving lizard. Its grayish to charcoal ground coloration blends almost imperceptibly with the hues of the granite boulders on which it dwells. It has a flattened body and head. Dark dorsal spots are often connected into a reticulum. The belly is white. A gular fold and a lateral fold are both present.

Similar species: This lizard is very similar in appearance to the Yucca night lizard (account 166). Use range as the primary identifying criterion.

Taxonomic comment: This night lizard is considered a subspecies of the desert (yucca) night lizard by some authorities.

ADDITIONAL SPECIES

As currently recognized, none.

Sierra night lizard. Photo by Tim Burkhardt

166. Desert (Yucca) Night Lizard

Xantusia vigilis vigilis

Abundance/Range: Al-though its range can be spotty, in most areas where it is found and when it is surface active, this is a very abundant lizard. However, it is so secre-tive that its presence is often unsuspected. It occurs in extreme southwesten Utah, southern Nevada, southern California, and north central Baja California.

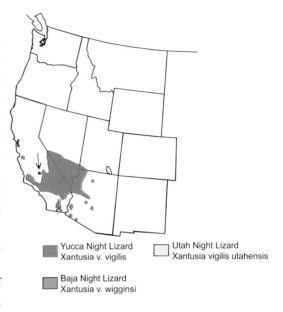

Yucca Night Lizard
Xantusia v. vigilis

Utah Night Lizard
Xantusia vigilis utahensis

Baja Night Lizard
Xantusia v. wigginsi

Habitat: The habitat of this lizard is very firmly associ-ated with the presence of dead and fallen Joshua trees and their limbs and to a lesser degree with other species of yuccas and agaves. The lizards thrive in the duff below the fallen vegetation and may

Yucca night lizard

also hide in the hollows of the dried limbs and flowerstalks themselves. In some regions desert night lizards may also be found in rock crevices, behind rock flakes, and in other such habitats.

Size: This is a tiny lizard. Adults are seldom more than 3½ inches in length, of which the tail is slightly more than half. Despite the small size of the adults, neonates are almost 2 inches in length.

Identifying features: This is a tiny, agile, and very fast-moving little lizard. Its back and sides are clad in scales of olive, tan, or olive to charcoal. There is commonly a peppering of very fine black dots, and a light dorsolateral line is usually visible on each side from the eye to midbody. The belly is white. A gular fold and a lateral fold are both present.

Similar species: Other species of night lizards have prominent dorsal and lateral flecking or spotting.

167. The disjunct population of small night lizards in southeastern Utah was long known as the Utah Night Lizard, *Xantusia vigilis utahensis*. Although this has recently been determined to be an invalid designation, we have elected to recognize it herein. This night lizard may be found in the nooks and crannies of the red sandstone cliffs. In keeping with the color of the rocks, the dorsal hues of this little lizard are orange, terra-cotta, or tan. It is apt to be paler on the sides. Besides the sandstone flakes and crevices, this night lizard may be found beneath dead yuccas, in packrat middens, and beneath rocks.

Utah night lizard

Baja night lizard

168. The population of yucca night lizards near Jacumba, California, has recently been revaluated and is now identified as *Xantusia vigilis wigginsi*, the Baja Night Lizard. The range of this race extends well southward into the Baja Peninsula. The lizards occur amid the dead yucca plants barely a stone's throw from the international boundary. The dorsum is often finely peppered with tiny, discrete, dark dots. If black spots are present on the tail, they are restricted to the tips of the scales. Some individuals are devoid of all spotting.

Glossary

Aestivation: A period of warm weather inactivity; often triggered by excessive heat or drought.

Ambient temperature: The temperature of the surrounding environment.

Anterior: Toward the front.

Anus: The external opening of the cloaca; the vent.

Arboreal: Tree-dwelling.

Autotomize: To break off/break free, such as the tail of a lizard.

Barbels: Downward-projecting papillae on the chin and/or throat of turtles. Commonly seen on musk and mud turtles.

Bridge: The area of a turtle's shell that connects the carapace to the plastron.

Brille: The transparent "spectacle" covering the eyes of a gecko or night lizard.

Brumation: The reptilian equivalent of hibernation.

Carapace: The top shell of a turtle

Caudal: Pertaining to the tail.

Cloaca: The common chamber into which digestive, urinary, and reproductive systems empty and which itself opens exteriorly through the vent or anus.

Crepuscular: Active at dusk and/or dawn.

Cusp: Downward projections, at both sides of a medial notch, on the upper mandible of red-bellied turtles.

Deposition: As used here, the laying of eggs or birthing of young.

Deposition site: The spot chosen by the female to lay her eggs or have young.

Dimorphism: A difference in form, build, or coloration involving the same species; often sex-linked.

Diurnal: Active in the daytime.

Dorsal: Pertaining to the back; upper surface.

Dorsolateral: Pertaining to the upper sides.

Dorsum: The upper surface.

Ecological niche: The precise habitat utilized by a species.

Ectothermic: "Cold-blooded"; pertaining to animals that absorb heat from the environment.

Endothermic: "Warm-blooded"; pertaining to animals that produce their own body heat.

Form: An identifiable species or subspecies.

Fossorial: Adapted for burrowing. Pertaining to a burrowing species.

Fracture plane: A weakened area of bone that permits a lizard's tail to readily autotomize.

Frontoparietal scale: The enlarged scale atop a lizard's head, between the frontal and parietal scales.

Genus, pl. genera: A taxonomic classification of a group of species having similar characteristics. The genus falls between the next higher designation of "family" and the next lower designation of "species." The genus name is always capitalized when written.

Glottis: The opening of the windpipe.

Granular: As used here, small, nonoverlapping scales of some lizards.

Gravidity: The reptilian equivalent of mammalian pregnancy.

Gular: Pertaining to the throat.

Gular fold: A fold of skin across the throat of many lizard species. Less well-defined folds may be present anterior to the main fold.

Heliothermic: Pertaining to a species that basks in the sun to thermoregulate.

Hemipenes: The dual copulatory organs of male lizards and snakes. Singular is hemipenis.

Herpetology: The study (often scientifically oriented) of reptiles and amphibians.

Hibernacula: Winter dens.

Hybrid: Offspring resulting from the breeding of two species or noncontiguous subspecies.

Insular: As used here, island-dwelling.

Intergrade: Offspring resulting from the breeding of two subspecies.

Interorbital: On the top of the head between the eyes.

Jacobson's organs: Highly innervated olfactory pits in the palate of snakes and lizards.

Juvenile: A young or immature specimen.

Keel: As used here, a ridge along the center of a scale.

Labial: Pertaining to the lips.

Lateral: Pertaining to the side.

Melanism: A profusion of black pigment.

Mental: The scale at the tip of the lower lip.

Mesoptychial scales: Those scales immediately anterior to the gular fold.

Metachrosis: The changing of color, often in response to climatic conditions or to photoperiod.

Middorsal: Pertaining to the middle of the back.

Midventral: Pertaining to the center of the belly or abdomen.

Monotypic: Containing but one type.

Nocturnal: Active at night.

Ontogenetic: Age-related (color) changes.

Oviparous: Reproducing by means of eggs that hatch after laying.

Ovoviviparous: Reproducing by means of shelled or membrane-contained eggs that hatch prior to, or at deposition.

Papillae: Fleshy, nipple-like projections on the necks of some turtles.

Paravertebral: Stripes, spots, or scales paralleling, but on each side of the vertebral line.

Photoperiod: The daily/seasonally variable length of the hours of daylight.

Plastron: The bottom shell of a turtle.

Pores: Circular or oval openings at the rear of the bridge scutes of some species of sea turtles.

Postantebrachial scales: Scales on the rear of the foreleg. These may or may not be be enlarged on whiptails and racerunners.

Postocular: Behind the eyes.

Race: A subspecies.

Rostral: The (often modified) scale on the tip of the snout.

Rugose: Not smooth; wrinkled or tuberculate.

Saxicolous: Rock-dwelling.

Scute: Scale. Usually referring to a large platelike scale, such as the belly scales of most snakes or on turtle's shells.

Species: A group of similar creatures that produce viable young when breeding. The taxonomic designation that falls beneath genus and above subspecies. Abbreviation, sp.; plural, spp.

Subocular: Beneath the eye.

Subspecies: The subdivision of a species. A race that may differ slightly in color, size, scalation, or other criteria. Abbreviation, ssp.

Supralabials: The scales edging the upper lip.

Supraoculars: The (often shieldlike) scales above the eyes.

Supraorbital semicircles: A grouping of small scales extending forward from the rear above the eye, partially or completely separating the frontoparietal scale(s) from the

supraoculars.

SVL or svl: Snout-vent length, a standard method of measuring amphibians and reptiles.

Sympatric: Occurring together.

Taxonomy: The science of classification of plants and animals.

Terrestrial: Land-dwelling.

Thermoregulate: To regulate (body) temperature externally by choosing a warmer or cooler environment.

Vent: The external opening of the cloaca; the anus.

Venter: The underside of a creature; the belly.

Ventral: Pertaining to the undersurface or belly.

Ventrolateral: Pertaining to the sides of the venter, or belly.

Acknowledgments

Many people helped with this book.

Brad Alexander, Robert Applegate, Abe Blank, Tim Burkhardt, Dennis Cathcart, Brian Crother, Harold DeLisle, Will Flaxington, Fred Gehlbach, Chris Gruenwald, Bob Hansen, Jim Harding, Pierson Hill, Andy Holycross, Richard Hoyer, Gerald Keown, Ken King, Jason Jones, Jeff Lemm, Randy Limburg, Sean McKeown, Josh McLane, Jim Melli, Gerold and Cindy Merker, Dennie Miller, Mitch Mulks, Regis Opferman, Ed Pirog, Gus Rentfro, Mark Robertson, Buzz Ross, Dan Scolaro, Brad Smith, Mike Souza, J. P. Stephenson, Karl Heinz-Switak, Ernie Wagner, Will Wells, and Anish Yelekar provided nomenclatural information, field information, companionship and hospitality during our travels.

Randy Babb, Jeff Boundy, Bob Hansen, Paul Moler, Charlie Painter, Tom Tyning, and Wayne Van Devender provided us with encouragement and challenges—encouragement for the task at hand, and challenges of actually finding some of the better field locations that they so generously shared and at which we eventually photographed. Randy Babb, Tim Burkhardt, Gary M. Fellers, Bob Hansen, Fred Kraus, Jeff Lemm, Gerald McCormack, Wendy McKeown, Gary Nafis, and Karl Heinz-Switak also provided us with photographs of taxa that evaded or avoided our field searches. Kenny Wray provided us with many illustrations.

Gordy Johnston introduced the wonders of the Chiricahuas to one of us more than five decades ago. Wade and Emily Sherbrooke, of the Southwest Research Station in Portal, Arizona, made it possible for others to explore and experience the Chiricahuas.

Chuck Hurt, Craig McIntyre, Bill Love, Chris McQuade, Rob MacInnes, Mike Stuhlman, and Eric Thiss extended to us the privilege of photographing reptiles and amphibians in their respective collections. Kenny Wray, Scott Cushnir, Pierson Hill, Randy Babb, and Gary Nafis were field companions par excellence.

References and Additional Reading

Bartlett, Richard D. 1988. *In Search of Reptiles and Amphibians*. Leiden: E. J. Brill.

Bartlett, Richard D., and Patricia Bartlett. 1999. *Terrarium and Cage Construction and Care*. Hauppauge, N.Y.: Barron's.

Bartlett, R. D., and Alan Tennant. 2000. *Snakes of North America: Western Region*. Houston, Tex.: Gulf Pub.

Baxter, George T., and Michael D. Stone. 1980. *Amphibians and Reptiles of Wyoming*. Cheyenne: Wyoming Game and Fish Department.

Behler, John L., and F. Wayne King. 1979. *National Audubon Society Field Guide to North American Reptiles and Amphibians*. New York: Alfred A. Knopf.

Brennan, T. C., and A. T. Holycross. 2006. *A Field Guide to Amphibians and Reptiles in Arizona*. Phoenix: Arizona Game and Fish Department.

———. 2005. *A Field Guide to Amphibians and Reptiles of Maricopa County*. Phoenix: Arizona Game and Fish Department.

Brown, David E., and Neil B. Carmony. 1991. *Gila Monster: Facts and Folklore of America's Aztec Lizard*. Silver City, N.Mex.: High Lonesome Books.

Brown, Vinson. 1974. *Reptiles and Amphibians of the West*. Happy Camp, Calif.: Naturegraph Pub.

Collins, Joseph T. 1982. *Amphibians and Reptiles in Kansas*. Lawrence: University of Kansas.

Conant, Roger, and Joseph T. Collins. 1998. *A Field Guide to Reptiles and Amphibians: Eastern and Central North America*, 3rd ed. Boston: Houghton Mifflin.

Crother, Brian I., Chair. 2000. Scientific and Standard English Names of Amphibians and Reptiles of North America North of Mexico, with Comments Regarding Confidence in Our Understanding. Herpetological Circular 29. St. Louis, Mo.: SSAR.

Degenhardt, William G., Charles W. Painter, and Andrew H. Price. 1996. *Amphibians and Reptiles of New Mexico*. Albuquerque: University of New Mexico Press.

Ernst, Carl H. 1992. *Venomous Reptiles of North America*. Washington, D.C.: Smithsonian Press.

Halliday, Tim R., and Kraig Adler, eds. 1987. *The Encyclopedia of Reptiles and Amphibians*. New York: Facts on File.

Hammerson, Geoffrey A. 1986. *Amphibians and Reptiles in Colorado*. Denver: Colorado Division of Wildlife.

Lemm, Jeffrey M. 2006. *Field Guide to the Amphibians and Reptiles of the San Diego Region*. Berkeley: University of California Press.

Lowe, Charles H., Cecil R. Schwalbe, and Terry B. Johnson. 1986. *The Venomous Reptiles of Arizona*. Phoenix: Arizona Fish and Game Department.

McKeown, Sean. 1996. *A Field Guide to Reptiles and Amphibians in the Hawaiian Islands*. Los Osos, Calif.: Diamond Head Pub.

Stebbins, Robert C. 2003. *A Field Guide to Western Reptiles and Amphibians*, 3rd ed. Boston: Houghton Mifflin.

Storm, Robert M. and William P. Leonard, eds. 1995. *Reptiles of Washington and Oregon*. Seattle: Seattle Audubon Society.

Werner, J. Kirwin, et al. 2004. *Amphibians and Reptiles of Montana*. Missoula, Mont.: Mountain Press.

SOME HELPFUL WEB SITES

www.californiaherps.com
www.utahherps.info
www.livingunderworld.org
www.reptilesofaz.com
www.kingsnake.com
www.fieldherpers.com
www.fieldherpforum.com

Index

R. D. Bartlett is a veteran herpetologist/herpetoculturist with more than forty years' experience in writing, photography, and educating people about reptiles and amphibians. He is the author of numerous books on the subject, including *Guide and Reference to the Snakes of Eastern and Central North America (North of Mexico)* (2005), *Guide and Reference to the Amphibians of Eastern and Central North America (North of Mexico)* (2006), and *Guide and Reference to the Crocodilians, Turtles, and Lizards of Eastern and Central North America (North of Mexico)* (2006). He is the founder of the Reptilian Breeding and Research Institute, a private facility dedicated to herpetofauna study and support.

Patricia P. Bartlett is a biologist/historian who grew up chasing lizards on the mesas in Albuquerque, New Mexico. Had there been Komodo dragons present, she would have chased them, too. She attended Colorado State University with the intention of becoming a veterinarian but found the world of journalism and writing about creatures too interesting to resist. She moved to Florida after graduation, in part because of the reptiles and amphibians found there. Her background includes book editing, magazine production, museum administration, and program administration for a university. She is the author of books on koi, rabbits, and sharks, and has co-authored some 54 titles on natural history and history.